INS[illegible]NAL SOCCER STORIES FOR KIDS

LIONEL ANDERSON

For Bailey so proud of you and excited to watch you Skyrocket and grow into the Superstar I know you are!

And for Rene, thank you for always being my rock, and such a supportive presence in my life always!

ALSO BY THE AUTHOR

Inspirational Basketball Stories For Kids

https://www.champlinks.com/sl/basketball/

Inspirational Hockey Stories For Kids

https://www.champlinks.com/sl/hockey/

Inspirational Football Stories For Kids

https://www.champlinks.com/sl/football/

CONTENTS

THE BEAUTIFUL GAME'S POWER TO INSPIRE

Get ready to feel your heart race and your spirit soar as we step onto the most magical field in sports—the incredible world of soccer! HIGH FIVE!

Oh boy, oh boy, you're about to discover why they call soccer "the beautiful game," and trust me, it's not about those fancy footwork moves (though they're pretty amazing!). It's about something WAY more powerful—the ability to turn ordinary moments into pure magic!

Picture a soccer ball rolling through the streets of Brazil, kicked by a barefoot kid who would go on to be named Pelé and then become the greatest player ever.

Or imagine a young Mia Hamm, practicing shots in her backyard, not knowing she'd inspire millions of girls to chase the soccer ball and their dreams!

That right there is the incredible power of soccer—it transforms everyday places into launching pads for greatness!

THE UNIVERSAL LANGUAGE OF SOCCER

You know what's super mind-blowing? Soccer speaks every language on Earth!

When a striker celebrates a goal, everyone understands that feeling of pure joy! When teammates hug after a victory, that emotion needs no translation!

And talk about a super-powered teaching tool! Want to learn geography? Let's track the World Cup across continents! Need help with physics? Check out the perfect curve of a free kick! Looking to boost your math skills? Watch how players calculate angles for the perfect pass!

It's a beautiful language, and we can all become fluent in it!

FROM BACKYARD TO WORLD CUP: CHAMPIONS IN THE MAKING

Here's something that'll blow your mind—every single soccer superstar started exactly where you are right now!

Lionel Messi? He was once a tiny kid who doctors said was too small to play. Cristiano Ronaldo? He used to kick a ball made of rolled-up socks!

These legends didn't start with stadiums full of screaming fans—they started with a dream in their hearts and determination in their souls. And guess what?

That very same championship spirit lives inside *YOU*! Oh yes, you have it all, right now!

LESSON—THE POWER OF INSPIRATION

Let's drop some solid truth bombs about inspiration—it's that magical spark that turns "maybe someday" into "watch this happen!" It's that electric feeling when you see someone score an impossible goal and think, "I'm gonna do that too!"

Listen up! These soccer stories are rocket fuel for your mind! When you're struggling with a tough problem, remind yourself how Pelé practiced with a grapefruit in the early days, until he got his hands on a real ball. When you face setbacks, think about how Megan Rapinoe turned criticism into motivation!

Here's a cool tip:

Want to make the lessons from this awesome book stick? Create your own "Championship Playbook":

- Set bold goals like Messi
- Practice with purpose like Ronaldo
- Lead with a heart like Rapinoe
- Never give up like Pelé

Check this out—when you learn how your soccer heroes overcame obstacles, suddenly your own challenges feel more manageable! That big test? It's your World Cup final! That difficult project? Time to show some teamwork magic!

Here's the real game-changer—these stories are blueprints for turning dreams into reality! Every pass, every goal, and every victory shows us that greatness isn't about where you start—it's about how much determination and perseverance you have for what you believe in to get where you're supposed to be! And, where are you supposed to be?

IN YOUR ULTIMATE GREATNESS!

Soccer isn't contained by stadium walls or limited by language barriers. It's a force that brings people together, ignites passion, and proves that anything is possible with enough boldness and belief!

And that's the true beauty of the beautiful game—it reminds us that champions aren't born wearing golden boots. They're built through countless hours of practice, unwavering dedication, and the courage to keep pushing when others might quit. So here's your challenge, future champions—take these stories and let them fuel your fire! Whether you dream of lifting the World Cup or achieving something completely different, remember that every legend started with a single step, a single kick, a single moment of believing in themselves!

Your story is waiting to be written, and the field of possibilities is wide open!

Every great achievement in history started with someone saying, "Why not me?" So grab your dreams with both hands, let your spirit soar, and get ready to show the world what you're made of!

Game on!

LIONEL MESSI AND TIM HOWARD

Ready to unlock the ultimate power move in sports? It's not a fancy trick or a secret technique—it's something even *MORE* powerful: the champion's mindset!

And boy, do I have two incredible heroes to show you how it's done!

Let's talk about what makes a champion's mindset so special. Imagine having a superpower that turns every challenge into an opportunity, every setback into a setup for a comeback! That's exactly what a positive mindset does—it transforms the way you see everything! Think of your mind like a soccer field—you can choose what to fill it with and you can create the perfect playing conditions for success! And nobody shows this better than our two soccer superstars, Lionel Messi and Tim Howard!

Let's look at the magical Messi! This guy? He's not thinking about scoring goals—he's creating art on the field! Every time he steps onto that pitch, he brings something special: pure joy! Watch him play, and you'll see someone who absolutely *LOVES* what he does. That smile when he's dribbling past defenders? That's your champion mindset in action! Messi shows us that greatness comes from believing in yourself and turning pressure into excitement! When others see obstacles, Messi sees opportunities. When others feel pressure, he feels possibility! That's the kind of mindset that turns good players into *LEGENDS*!

Now, check out Tim Howard—talk about a wall of positive energy in goal! This goalkeeper extraordinaire shows us that mindset isn't about never facing tough shots—it's about being ready for anything that comes your way! Howard approaches every game with incredible focus and determination, turning saves into statements!

Here's what makes these champions truly special—they don't wait for perfect conditions to shine. They *CREATE* their own sunshine! Every practice, every game, every moment is a chance to prove that mindset beats circumstance every single time!

Want to build your own champion's mindset? Let's take a quick look at what's on the menu:

- See challenges as chances to grow stronger
- Focus on what you *CAN* control
- Celebrate small wins along the way
- Stay positive, especially when things get tough
- Surround yourself with supporters who believe in you

The most amazing part? This mindset magic works everywhere—on the field, in the classroom, and in life! When you face a tough test? Channel your inner Messi and approach it with confidence! Dealing with a challenging situation? Think like Howard and stay focused on your goals!

Messi and Howard didn't become legends because everything was perfect. They became legends because they chose to see possibilities where others saw problems!

So what's it gonna be, superstar? Are you ready to upgrade your mindset and unleash your inner champion? The field is yours, the moment is now, and your positive mindset is what's going to help you shine!

LIONEL MESSI

Hey there, champion! Let me have the honor of properly introducing you to someone totally epic—the magical LIONEL MESSI!

You know what's incredible about Messi? When people looked at him, they saw a kid who was smaller than everyone else on the field. But when Messi looked in the mirror? He saw a *GIANT*! That's right—while others focused on his size, he focused on his *SUPERSIZED* dreams!

Did you know Messi's first contract with Barcelona was signed on a *NAPKIN*? Yep, you read that right! Picture this: a 13-year-old boy, sitting in a restaurant, while club officials scrambled to find anything they could write on because they knew they were in the presence of someone special. That napkin? It might've been paper, but it was worth its weight in gold! And talk about believing in yourself—when everyone said "too small," Messi said, "Watch this!" He turned his size into his superpower! Being smaller meant he could turn faster, squeeze through tight spaces, and zigzag past defenders like they were standing still!

BOOM! That's what happens when you flip the script on your challenges and turn them into advantages!

Here's something that'll make you say "*AWESOME!*"—the legendary Diego Maradona himself looked at Messi and said, "That's my successor right there!" Think about that—one of the greatest players *EVER* picked Messi to carry on his legacy. And guess what? Messi didn't crack under that pressure—he freaking *SOARED*!

Want to know Messi's secret?

It's his mindset! Every time he steps onto that field, he's not thinking about being the best—he's thinking about being *BETTER* than he was yesterday!

That's how you build greatness, one day at a time!

TIM HOWARD

And now, let me introduce you to another absolute legend—TIM HOWARD, the wall of pure awesomeness in goal!

Listen to this quote from Howard that'll fire you up: "What I've learned, really, is that you've got to believe in what you can do. And then you've got to work like crazy to make it happen." BAM! That's champion talk right there!

Howard didn't become a goalkeeping genius by accident—he *CHOSE* to be incredible! Every single day, he showed up ready to stop any shot that came his way. But here's what makes him truly special—he didn't wait for confidence to find him, he *BUILT* it, save by save, game by game!

Do you want to talk about self-belief?

Howard stepped onto the biggest stages in soccer—the English Premier League, the World Cup—and played like he *OWNED* that goal! He didn't hope to make saves; he *EXPECTED* to make them! Howard holds the record for most saves in a World Cup match with 16 stops against Belgium in 2014! That's what happens when you combine incredible skill with unshakeable belief in yourself! Here's what makes Howard's story even more amazing—he turned pressure into power! When the lights were brightest and the stakes were highest, that's when he shined the most! Why? Because he trained his mind to be as strong as his skills!

The coolest part about Howard's mindset?

He showed us that confidence isn't about never making mistakes—it's about knowing that no mistake can define you! Every time he got scored on, he bounced back stronger. That's not talent—that's pure rock solid mental strength!

So here's what you can learn from these legends: Messi taught us that your size doesn't determine your impact—your *MINDSET* does! And Howard showed us that believing in yourself isn't being cocky—it's being *READY* for greatness!

You can have and be anything in life. But, you have to get out there and earn it, claim it, and own it!

You've got your own kind of magic waiting to shine! How cool is that? Whether you're small like Messi or bold like Howard, your mindset is your superpower!

The field is calling your name, champion! Time to write your legend!

LESSONS: YOUR MAGICAL BRAIN

Let me tell you something amazing—your brain is like a magical muscle that gets stronger every single time you push yourself to learn something new!

Do you know what the brilliant Dr. Carol Dweck discovered? She found out there are two types of mindsets: fixed and growth. And here's the exciting part—*YOU* get to choose which one you want! When you pick that growth mindset, you're telling yourself, "I can learn anything! I can improve! I can become better!" How amazing is that?

Let's talk about Messi and Howard, again! These superstars didn't wake up one day being awesome at their sport. Nope! They built their success piece by piece, practice by practice, believing in themselves every step of the way! Take Messi—this soccer wizard wasn't born scoring spectacular goals. He faced challenges that could have stopped him in his tracks. But you know what made him unstoppable? His incredible belief in himself and his dedication to getting better every single day! He once said, "You have to fight to reach your dream. You have to sacrifice and work hard for it."

And Tim Howard? This goalkeeping genius shows us exactly what James Clear talks about in "Atomic Habits"—it's those tiny improvements, those daily habits that add up to something spectacular! Howard made saving goals look easy because he practiced the same moves thousands of times until they became second nature!

Now, have you ever heard of the "flow state"? It's like having your very own superpower! Athletes call it being "in the zone"—when everything clicks and you're performing at your absolute best. It's so awesome that it feels like you're even losing track of time! You're in your own world, a world of total awesomeness!

Whether you're practicing sports, studying for a test, or learning a new skill, you can tap into this incredible state of focus and excellence!

Want to know another powerful secret these athletes use? Visualization! Picture this: before every game, these champions close their eyes and see themselves succeeding. They imagine every move, every victory, every celebration. It's like creating your own epic movie! And guess what? This actually helps your brain prepare for real success!

Let's make this success thing totally crystal clear with some power moves you can start *TODAY*:

- **Champion Morning Routine**
  - Wake up and give yourself a high five in the mirror
  - Say out loud: "I'm getting stronger and better every day!"
  - Write down THREE things you're excited to learn today
  - Take 5 deep breaths and picture yourself being amazing

- **Visualization Power Up**
    - Find a quiet spot (your personal success zone!)
    - Close your eyes and breathe slowly
    - Picture yourself doing something awesome in SUPER detail
        i. What are you wearing?
        ii. How do you feel?
        iii. What sounds do you hear?
        iv. See yourself succeeding with a big smile!
    - Do this for 5 minutes before practice or studying
- **Get in the Zone—Flow State**
    - Pick *ONE* thing to focus on (no multitasking!)
    - Set a timer for 25 minutes
    - Turn off your phone (those TikToks can wait!)
    - Create your perfect focus space
    - Put on music that pumps you up
    - Start with something challenging but not too hard
- **Growth Mindset Power Words**
    - Instead of saying: "I can't do this!"
    - → Say: "I can't do this YET!"
    - "This is too hard!"
    - → Say: "This is my chance to grow!"
    - "I made a mistake!"
    - → Say: "Look what I can learn from this!"

- **Daily Habit Heroes**
  - Start TINY! Want to get better at soccer? Start with 10 shots on goal every day
  - Same time, same place (your brain loves routine!)
  - Track your progress in a fun notebook with stickers
  - Celebrate every single win, no matter how small
  - Stack habits: "After I brush my teeth, I'll read one page"
- **Self-Belief Boosters**
  - Create a "Win Wall" in your room
  - Write down every tiny victory
  - Take pictures of your progress
  - Keep a "My Awesome Moments" journal
  - Share your goals with your biggest supporters
- **When Things Get Tough**
  - Take a deep breath
  - Say "I can handle this!"
  - Break big challenges into tiny baby steps
  - Ask for help (even champions have coaches!)
  - Remember a time you did something hard before
- **Bring it To School**
  - Before tests: Close your eyes, see yourself staying calm, and crushing it
  - Homework time: Set up your success space
  - Learning something new? Say "My brain is growing stronger!"
  - Stuck on a problem? Channel Messi's persistence!

These strategies work for everything! Got a big test coming up? Visualize yourself staying calm and answering questions confidently. Want to learn a new instrument? Break it down into small, daily practice sessions. Remember, every expert started as a beginner!

Your positive mindset is your secret superpower!

When you believe in yourself and your ability to grow, you become unstoppable. Every time you face a challenge, tell yourself, "I can learn from this. I can get better. I've got this!"

Remember what Lionel Messi said: "Everything is possible in this life if you never stop believing in yourself and in your dreams." That's your new power phrase, champion!

Your journey to greatness starts right now, with one simple choice—choosing to believe in yourself and your ability to grow. You're not only capable of amazing things—you're made for them!

HEY SPORTS FANS!

I wanted to say welcome to this world of Inspirational Sports Stories for Kids!

As a thank you for becoming one of our readers, I've put together some amazing gifts for you.

By scanning the QR code or clicking the link (If you are reading the eBook) below, you will gain access to:

- **Positive Mindset for Young Champions** — Master the mental game and train your brain like a pro.
- **Sports Snapshots: Fun Facts for Young Champions** — Discover amazing and unexpected facts about the sports you love.
- **3 Free Soccer Drill Videos** — Taught by a Young American Pro playing for Inter Barcelona FC in Spain– Easy to Follow to Boost Your Skills Fast!

So go ahead and scan this QR code and take your love for sports to the next level.

Lionel

Keep playing, keep dreaming, and always have fun!

https://www.champlinks.com/sl/freebonuses/

JAMAL MUSIALA AND CHRISTIAN PULISIC

OH WOW! Imagine this mind-blowing truth bomb: Some soccer heroes start crushing it before most kids even get their driver's licenses! We're talking about incredible young athletes who turn soccer fields into launching pads for EPIC life adventures!

Take Kylian Mbappé, he scored his first professional goal at 16 and became a World Cup champion at 19! How's that for smashing age barriers? These young soccer wizards are rewriting the entire rulebook of possibility!

Power Lesson 101: Age is just a number, and potential has no boundaries!

When young stars shine bright, they explode onto the scene! Erling Haaland was scoring professional goals at 16. Pedri was a Barcelona regular at 17. These are more than athletes, they are dream architects building their futures one incredible play at a time! But here's the super-important truth: Early success isn't about scoring goals. It's about MASSIVE life skills training! These young champions learn discipline that most adults can only dream about. Imagine practicing for hours after school, balancing intense training with homework, and managing global expectations—all while most teenagers are figuring out how to get homework done!

Let's drop some serious wisdom about something I like to call "the discipline diamond:" The skills these young soccer stars develop are way more than soccer skills. They're life skills! We're talking:

- Rock solid time management
- Confidence that could move mountains
- Understanding teamwork like true champions
- Handling responsibility that would make grown-ups sweat

Every practice and every game becomes a masterclass in personal growth. These are future leaders learning to conquer challenges far beyond their years!

Sure, young soccer stars face massive challenges. Pressure? They eat it for breakfast! Media attention? They surf those waves like champions! While most teenagers worry about who thinks they're cute, these athletes are negotiating contracts and representing global brands! But here's the magic of this scenario—these experiences are about building unshakeable confidence. When you've scored a goal in front of 80,000 fans before turning 20, what CAN'T you do?

So, want to unlock your own potential? Here's a sneak peek at your game plan:

- Set bold goals
- Practice with purpose
- Learn from every single moment
- Never, ever give up!

Remember: Every soccer legend started exactly where you are right now—with a dream, determination, and the courage to take that first kick!

Soccer teaches us something mind-blowing: Your age doesn't define your potential. Your passion does! Whether you dream of World Cup glory or creating your own path, these young soccer stars prove one thing—GREATNESS has NO AGE BARRIER!

The field of possibilities? Wide open! So grab those dreams, let your spirit soar, and get ready to show the world exactly what you're made of!

JAMAL MUSIALA

When soccer dreams collide with mind-blowing talent, you get Jamal Musiala—a young star who's revolutionizing how we see soccer icons!

Musiala's journey through Bayern Munich's youth system reads like an epic adventure novel! Imagine being so incredible that professional scouts are tracking your every move before you're even old enough to vote! From his first steps in the academy, he was a future legend waiting to explode!

Born in Stuttgart, and raised with a global perspective, Musiala represents a new generation of soccer champions who break every single expectation! His path was about more than kicking a ball—it was about creating a new soccer narrative. Here's a mind-blowing decision that would make most teenagers panic: choosing between international soccer representation for England or Germany. Most people would see this as a challenge. Musiala? He saw an opportunity!

Growing up with roots in both countries, he brought a unique perspective that made soccer executives sit up and take notice! His decision to represent Germany was about honoring his heritage and showing the world what true soccer passion looks like! While most teenagers are stuck in high school drama, Musiala was dominating professional soccer fields with a maturity that defies his age! His playing style? It's like watching a soccer genius paint a masterpiece with his feet!

Quick thinking, lightning-fast moves, and a basketball-like court vision that makes veteran players look like they're standing still—that's the Jamal Musiala magic!

He reads the game like a grandmaster reads a chess board, anticipating moves before they even happen!

But Musiala's success is about crazy-awesome continuous learning! Every training session is a chance to grow, to improve, to become even more incredible. He approaches each practice like a scientist approaches an experiment—curious, focused, always looking to understand something new! While other players see limitations, Musiala sees endless possibilities!

Imagine the pressure of representing Bayern Munich and the German national team before you're 21! Most people would crumble. Musiala? He THRIVES under pressure like a diamond being formed! His ability to maintain composure, make split-second decisions, and deliver when it matters most separates him from ordinary players. Transitioning from youth to senior-level soccer isn't a stepping stone—it's a Quantum leap! Musiala redefined what adaptation looks like! He absorbed techniques, learned from veterans, and quickly became a player other athletes studied. His tactical intelligence allows him to play multiple positions, which broke down opposing teams' defensive strategies! One moment he's a midfielder, the next he's creating scoring opportunities that seem impossible!

Musiala proves one epic truth: Success isn't about where you start. It's about your hunger to improve, your courage to take risks, and your commitment to your dreams!

His journey screams a message to every young dreamer: Your potential has NO LIMITS! Whether you're dreaming of soccer glory or creating your own path in another field, remember—greatness starts with believing in yourself:

- Embrace every single challenge
- Learn from every moment
- Believe in yourself more than anyone else does
- Never, ever stop growing

The soccer world admires Jamal Musiala greatly and watches him in awe! He's a totally amazing role model and young sports hero!!

That's how legends are born—one incredible kick at a time!

CHRISTIAN PULISIC

Get ready to meet the soccer superstar who turned the American dream into a global reality!

Christian Pulisic: The American soccer rocket launching dreams!

Picture a kid from Hershey, Pennsylvania—a place more famous for chocolate than soccer—who would become the ultimate game-changer for U.S. soccer! Christian Pulisic is a living, breathing soccer revolution! Imagine being so incredible that professional teams are watching your every move from the start of your soccer journey! Pulisic's journey from small-town Pennsylvania to the massive soccer stages of Borussia Dortmund is the kind of story that makes your heart swell with inspiration!

At just 16 years old, while most teenagers were going to high school dances, Pulisic was dominating soccer fields in Germany! When he moved to Europe, he conquered it! The soccer world watched in total amazement as this young American turned heads left and right!

Here's a mind-blowing challenge—being labeled "Captain America" of soccer! Most people would crumble under such massive expectations. But Pulisic? He embraced it like a true champion! Suddenly, he was carrying the hopes of an entire nation's soccer dreams. Imagine the pressure of being the face of U.S. soccer on global stages! While other players might shrink, Pulisic expanded his game, showing the world that American soccer players could be just as talented as the top soccer nations!

When Pulisic hit the Bundesliga, he conducted it like a maestro! Quick moves, lightning-fast thinking, and a skill set that made veteran players look twice—he was rewriting the script of what an American soccer player could be. Every match became a statement. Every goal was a message to the world: U.S. soccer has arrived, and we're not only participating—we're here to stay!

Most people would melt under the weight of being a national sports icon. But Pulisic transformed those expectations into rocket fuel! He understood that being "Captain America" was a responsibility to inspire an entire generation. Young soccer players across the U.S. suddenly saw a living example of what's possible. Pulisic was building dreams for millions of kids who now believed they could compete on the world stage!

Here's the super-secret of Pulisic's success: He NEVER stops improving! While others might rest on their achievements, he treats every training session like a championship-winning opportunity!

Imagine approaching your passion with such crazy-awesome commitment that improvement becomes your daily mission! That's the Pulisic way—turning challenges into opportunities, setbacks into comebacks. Pulisic did more than score goals. He shattered cultural perceptions about American soccer! In a sport dominated by European and South American talents, he proved that soccer greatness can come from anywhere!

His journey showed young athletes that your location doesn't define your potential. Your passion, dedication, and willingness to work hard do!

Every time Pulisic steps on the field, he's igniting dreams for countless young soccer players! He proves that with enough determination, you can turn small-town dreams into global achievements!

- Embrace every challenge like it's your championship moment
- Learn from every single experience
- Believe in yourself more than anyone else does
- Never, ever stop growing

Christian Pulisic proves one epic thing: Your origins don't define your destination. Your determination does!

Whether you dream of soccer glory or creating your own path, remember—greatness starts with believing in yourself! Every soccer legend started exactly where you are right now—with a dream, determination, and the desire to take that first kick!

The field of possibilities? Wide open! So grab those dreams, let your spirit soar, and get ready to show the world exactly what you're made of!

LESSON: UNLEASHING YOUR INNER GREATNESS!

Imagine cracking the code to success before most kids go to prom! Jamal Musiala and Christian Pulisic are living, breathing blueprints of how to crush life's challenges!

These two athletes strategically shaped their destiny with every decision, every practice, every single drill. I'm about to break down their secrets for you. No magic wands here, only pure, relentless determination, combined with a mindset so powerful it makes everything else seem like a mere side hustle!

THE MINDSET MAGIC: MORE THAN JUST A GAME

Discipline isn't about punishment. It's about power! Think of your mind like a super-charged soccer field where every thought is a potential goal-scoring opportunity!

Every time you make a decision, you're either setting yourself up for a winning shot or a missed opportunity. And guess what? These young soccer wizards—Musiala and Pulisic—show us that true greatness starts between your ears. The magic lies in the way you shape your mindset. They don't only get out there and play the game; they transform it. These athletes are not defined by their circumstances; they're defined by how they choose to respond to challenges. Every moment of adversity becomes a stepping stone, not a roadblock.

When expectations feel like mountain-sized challenges, Musiala and Pulisic transform them into launching pads! Most teenagers would freak out under global pressure. But these champions? They turn expectations into rocket fuel for their dreams! That's the kind of mindset we're talking about—seeing obstacles not as walls but as ramps to your success.

What feels like an insurmountable mountain is actually an invitation to climb higher and reach further.

Navigating the Pressure Playground

Picture this: you're 18 years old, with millions watching every single move. Sounds terrifying, right?

Not for our soccer heroes! They've mastered the ultimate life skill—staying cool when the world is watching! The cameras? They don't make Pulisic or Musiala nervous. The stadiums? They thrive in them. Their secret? They've learned to make pressure their ally, not their enemy. Instead of trembling under it, they use it to sharpen their focus, to fuel their desire to push past their limits.

When you're under the spotlight, the pressure can either make you or break you. These champions chose to let it make them. They didn't let it shrink them down—they expanded under it, growing in ways most people couldn't even imagine. And it's not because they don't feel fear. It's because they're willing to feel it, own it, and use it to perform at their best.

Specific Champion Strategies

Emotional control is your secret tool in your toolbelt. These young athletes teach us that staying calm isn't about never feeling nervous.

It's about dancing with those nerves and turning them into pure performance magic! The pressure doesn't go away—but you can choose how you react to it. This is where true champions shine: they don't freeze. They breathe. They think. And they act. Emotional control isn't about suppressing fear, anger, or stress. It's about channeling those emotions into something powerful—like a soccer player channeling adrenaline into a game-winning goal.

Want to handle massive expectations? Here's the game plan:

- **Treat challenges like exciting opportunities**—When you see a challenge as a chance to grow, it doesn't feel like a burden. It becomes an invitation to level up.
- **Practice self-talk that pumps you up**—The words you say to yourself shape your reality. Use empowering language that fuels your fire.
- **Break big goals into tiny, conquerable missions**—Don't look at the whole mountain; focus on the next step. Tackling a project or goal one small piece at a time makes it all feel doable.
- **Celebrate every single step of progress**—Small wins matter! Don't wait until the finish line to give yourself credit. Every milestone is a victory!

Academic Awesomeness Meets Soccer Strategy

The same skills that make Musiala a midfield genius? They'll CRUSH your school challenges!

Imagine approaching a tough math test with the same focus you'd use to score a championship-winning goal! The way Musiala anticipates the next move, reads the game, and positions himself for success on the field?

You can apply that same strategic thinking to anything in your life. A challenging project? The steps are clear if you approach it like a soccer play—break it down, focus on your strategy, and execute with precision.

Real-World Champion Translation:

School project feeling overwhelming? Break it down like a soccer play! Plan your approach, practice consistently, and visualize success! The best athletes in the world didn't get there by winging it. They planned. They practiced. And most importantly, they envisioned victory. Your brain is the most powerful muscle you've got—train it like a champion! The more you flex those mental muscles, the stronger you become.

Responsibility: Your Superpower

Most people see responsibility as a boring adult thing. Champions see it as their ultimate growth opportunity!

Pulisic didn't only represent himself when he played—he carried the hopes of an entire nation! He felt the weight of the world on his shoulders, but instead of letting it break him, he used it to rise higher. He didn't see it as pressure. He saw it as an opportunity to prove his mettle.

Talk about turning pressure into pure magic!

Embrace responsibility. Whether it's in sports, work, school, or life in general—being responsible doesn't mean simply being reliable. It means taking ownership of your journey. It's about saying, "This is MY path, and I'm going to own every step of it." Musiala and Pulisic don't shy away from their role.

They face their responsibility head-on, making the most of every opportunity they're given. That's the true definition of personal empowerment.

Emotional Intelligence: The Ultimate Skill

Understanding your emotions is like having a GPS for life's most complex challenges! Musiala understood the game and also his inner world—and that's how he controls the game. Emotional intelligence is the ability to recognize, understand, and manage your emotions. When you master emotional intelligence, you get to decide how you respond to the world around you, rather than immediately reacting.

Learning to understand and manage your feelings is like having a cheat code for success! The next time you face a tough situation, instead of letting stress take over, tap into that emotional control. Recognize what you're feeling, acknowledge it, and choose how you'll respond. You're in control, not your emotions.

Practical Growth Strategies

Want to level up your life? Here's how the champions do it:

- **Create a personal development playbook**—Champions don't leave their success to chance. They have a plan. Write down what you're working towards, track your progress, and make sure you're always moving forward.
- **Set crystal-clear goals**—Vague goals are like trying to score In a game without a net. Make them specific, measurable, and achievable.
- **Track your progress like a detective** —Evaluate your growth regularly. Are you on track? Are there adjustments to be made?
- **Embrace feedback as your best friend**—Feedback isn't criticism. It's information that can help you get better. Be open to it, and use it to improve.
- **Never, ever stop learning**—Champions are lifelong learners. There's always room to grow, to improve, to evolve. Never stop sharpening your skills.

The Continuous Growth Mindset

Early success isn't the destination—it's the starting line! Musiala and Pulisic prove that true champions are always hungry to improve! Every single day is a chance to become a better version of yourself. Success isn't a finish line; it's a continual journey. These two athletes didn't stop when they reached the top. They kept pushing. And that's what sets them apart.

Whether you dream of soccer glory, academic excellence, or creating your own unique path, remember this: your potential has no limits! Success isn't about being perfect. It's about being brave enough to keep growing! Your championship journey is uniquely yours.

The steps might look different for you than they did for Musiala and Pulisic, but the mindset is the same: Go all in, learn from every experience, and never stop striving for greatness.

Practical Application Checklist:

- Treat every challenge as a growth opportunity
- Develop a bulletproof belief in yourself
- Practice emotional intelligence daily
- Stay curious and hungry for knowledge
- Support and lift others on their journey

Age is just a number when you've got passion, dedication, and an unstoppable growth mindset! Musiala and Pulisic didn't become champions overnight. They became champions with every single choice, every practice, every moment of determination! You don't need to be born with some secret talent to succeed. You need the willingness to work, to learn, and to grow.

Your Championship Playbook Summary:

- Embrace challenges like they're your best friends
- Learn from every single moment
- Believe in yourself more than anyone else does
- Never, ever stop growing

Imagine yourself as the hero of your own story! These soccer legends started exactly where you are right now—ready and willing to take that first step!

So grab those dreams, let your spirit soar, and get ready to WIN at life!

DIEGO MARADONA AND JOHAN CRUYFF

Okay, get ready to EXPLODE your mind with the magic of soccer creativity! Imagine soccer as the most awesome canvas where athletes paint mind-blowing masterpieces with their feet! This is a magical world where imagination transforms everything! Soccer isn't about following rules—it's about shattering them! Every incredible play is like a lightning bolt of pure human creativity.

When players dance around defenders, they're creating living art!

Picture Lionel Messi weaving through defenders like a wizard casting spells. Each move isn't only about technique—it's pure imagination made visible! These soccer artists don't play the game; they REINVENT it with every single touch!

Creative players are like musical composers, but instead of instruments, they use their bodies! A perfectly timed pass is a stroke of genius! When a player sees a possibility that nobody else sees, they're doing something extraordinary! Most people see obstacles. Creative soccer champions see opportunities. When traditional strategies fail, imagination becomes the ultimate weapon! These players understand that rules are suggestions, and creativity is the real game-changer!

Soccer creativity isn't confined to the field. It's a life skill that transforms everything! Learning to think differently, to see solutions where others see challenges—that's the real championship mindset. Imagine approaching your math homework like a soccer play. Suddenly, complex problems become exciting puzzles waiting to be solved! Creative thinking means turning challenges into exciting adventures!

The magic of creativity extends *way* beyond soccer! The same brain that designs an incredible goal can solve complex scientific problems, create breathtaking art, or develop world-changing technologies!

Every soccer legend proves one epic truth: Innovation isn't about having all the answers. It's about being brave enough to ask wild questions and chase impossible dreams!

Want to unlock your creative superpowers? Here's how soccer legends do it:

- Embrace unexpected solutions
- See challenges as exciting puzzles
- Trust your instincts
- Practice thinking differently
- Never fear making mistakes

When Neymar makes an impossible move, he's showing the world that creativity has NO LIMITS! These players teach us that true greatness comes from seeing the world differently!

Think soccer creativity is all about sports? Wrong! It's about training your brain to see possibilities others miss! Approach your studies like a creative soccer play—be bold, be unexpected, be awesome! Creativity isn't a talent. It's a muscle you can train! Every time you think differently, you're becoming more powerful! Soccer shows us that imagination is the most incredible superpower humans possess.

Whether you dream of soccer glory or creating something entirely new, remember: your potential has no boundaries. Creativity is about believing in your unique vision! Age doesn't define creativity. Passion does! Every incredible achievement started with someone seeing the world differently.

That's how creative champions are born—one mind-blowing moment at a time!

DIEGO MARADONA

Imagine a player so incredible that he transformed the sport completely! Diego Maradona was a once-in-a-generation miracle who turned the soccer field into his personal magic carpet!

Born in the rough neighborhoods of Argentina, Maradona was challenging entire systems that said he was too small, too different to succeed! But here's the mind-blowing truth: He turned every single limitation into his ultimate superpower!

Smaller than most players, with feet that moved like lightning and a brain that saw possibilities nobody else could imagine, Maradona became a living legend! He proved that soccer isn't about size—it's about heart, creativity, and unstoppable determination. When Maradona stepped onto the field, something magical happened! Defenders who looked like giants suddenly became confused puppets. He danced around opponents! His body became a complete soccer instrument, telling stories with every single movement.

Imagine having the ability to change an entire game's direction with only one play! Most players dream of such power. Maradona lived it! He could transform hopeless situations into championship moments faster than you could blink.

While other players followed tactical rules, Maradona rewrote them. He saw soccer fields as blank canvases where he could paint impossible masterpieces! Every touch of the ball was like a musical note in a symphony of pure soccer genius. His playing style was about inspiring millions! Young players would watch him and suddenly believe that anything was possible! He showed the world that soccer is an art form where imagination rules supreme.

Most players saw defenders as obstacles. Maradona saw them as challenges waiting to be conquered! He could read the field like a grandmaster reads a chessboard, always three moves ahead of everyone else.

His brain worked differently. Where others saw closed doors, he saw secret passages. Physical limitations? He turned them into advantages that left entire teams scrambling to keep up. More than a player, Maradona became a national symbol! In Argentina, he was a representation of hope, passion, and the extraordinary potential of ordinary people! He showed that dreams have no boundaries.

Young soccer players wanted to become Maradona. He inspired an entire generation to believe in themselves, to chase impossible dreams, and to never, ever give up. Maradona understood something epic about soccer: It's 90% mental and 10% physical! While others relied on pure strength, he used intelligence, creativity, and an unbreakable spirit to dominate games.

His ability to read opponents, to understand exactly what they would do before they did it, was like having a superpower! When he orchestrated soccer plays, he conducted them like a musical maestro.

Maradona's impact went way beyond goals and championships! He showed the world that true greatness comes from believing in yourself more than anyone else does! His journey proved that your background doesn't define your potential—your passion and determination do!

Every time he stepped on the field, Maradona made history through the attitude he brought with him. He was proof that greatness doesn't land in your lap but comes from an unyielding will to make the impossible happen.

Want to unlock your inner Maradona? Here's how champions think:

- See challenges as exciting opportunities
- Trust your unique abilities
- Never let anyone limit your dreams
- Practice with purpose
- Believe in yourself more than anyone else

Want to succeed like the legend? Take risks. Go beyond the ordinary. Make people question what's possible. Take a page from Maradona's book—nothing extraordinary happens by playing it safe!

Diego Maradona proves one epic thing: Greatness isn't about being perfect. It's about being brave enough to be completely yourself! His genius wasn't about flawless play; it was about the fearless creativity he unleashed every time he touched the ball. Whether you dream of soccer glory or creating your own path, remember—greatness starts with believing in yourself.

Every legend started exactly where you are right now—with a dream, determination, and the desire to take that first kick! It's the bravery to pursue something audacious that sparks greatness, and it's that drive that powers your journey too.

Let's be real: passion is the game-changer. Maradona didn't let anything stop him from pursuing his passion, and his heart was the most powerful thing he had on his side. Passion doesn't follow the rules—it smashes them! Like Maradona did on the field, let your passion be the thing that defines your greatness. The more you believe in your drive and purpose, the more the world will make way for you. If your goals seem wild and unachievable, that's exactly how they should feel. Remember: The greatest achievements often start with an idea that sounds insane. But passion gives you the strength to prove the world wrong.

Maradona played the mental game better than anyone. He had a sharpness that allowed him to anticipate plays and read opponents like no one else. He was able to see what others couldn't—and that's what separated him from the rest.

The secret to Maradona's genius was his mental game. In soccer, as in life, you don't need to be the biggest or the strongest. What you need is the ability to think in ways that others can't even imagine. The soccer field is like life: it's not about how much you've got physically; it's about how you use what you have. Maradona's ability to outthink his competition is the stuff of legends. And you can tap into this power too—by learning to think differently, by always looking for the untapped opportunity, and by keeping your head in the game.

His influence reached far beyond the soccer world. He became a global symbol of resilience, showing that no matter where you come from, you can rise to greatness. His story reminds us that the class you were born into doesn't determine your destiny—your choices and beliefs do.

He broke through societal limitations. He defied expectations and showed the world that talent, combined with relentless passion and creativity, can create something truly unforgettable. He proved that greatness is born from a relentless refusal to be ordinary.

Maradona is about life and legacy. Whether you dream of dominating the soccer field or creating your own path, remember: The most important thing is to stay true to who you are. Maradona didn't conform. He redefined greatness by playing his way, with heart, with passion, and with creativity.

So, what's stopping you?

JOHAN CRUYFF

Imagine a player so incredible that he completely reinvented how the game was understood! Johan Cruyff was a pure genius!

He was a thinking revolution who transformed soccer from a simple sport into a complex, beautiful science! Cruyff didn't play the game to fit in with the norms of his time—he played to tear down every expectation and build something entirely new. His name is synonymous with brilliance, and a whole new way of thinking about soccer, leadership, and life itself.

Born in Amsterdam in 1947, Cruyff wasn't any ol' player. He was a genius with a vision so clear that he could see soccer not only as a game, but as a living, breathing organism, with intricate moves, opportunities, and patterns. To Johan, the soccer field was a chessboard, with every move telling a story, with every pass and dribble making the difference between brilliance and mediocrity. From his earliest days at Ajax to his legendary career at Barcelona and beyond, Cruyff revolutionized it, changing the way we all see and play soccer today.

Picture a world where soccer players weren't confined to rigid positions. Where defenders didn't just defend, midfielders didn't just pass, and attackers didn't just score goals. In Johan's world, every player was a multi-dimensional force, able to shift and change roles at will. This was Total Football, and Cruyff was its ULTIMATE architect.

Cruyff's soccer philosophy broke down the walls that restricted creativity on the field. He introduced a radical new concept where fluidity and intelligence reigned supreme. In this system, players were encouraged to express themselves freely and to see the whole field as their playground. Everyone had to think, move, and adapt with lightning speed. There were no "safe" positions, no "I'm just a defender" mentality. Every player was empowered to control the game in a way that was previously unthinkable.

It was this ability to think and act in multiple dimensions that set Cruyff apart. While others saw soccer as a set of rigid roles and predictable patterns, Cruyff saw a canvas, ready to be painted with creativity. And when he took his ideas from Ajax to Barcelona, the world watched in awe as his philosophy transformed the way soccer was played. Teams stopped being about individuals and started being about collective intelligence. It was no longer enough to be good with the ball—you had to think like a chess master, always several moves ahead of the opposition.

Let's talk about the most mind-blowing soccer move in history—the Cruyff Turn. This was no ordinary dribble. It was a game-changer. The Cruyff Turn was a complete reimagining of how a player could move with a soccer ball. When Cruyff did this signature move, defenders got tricked and outsmarted. They were left scrambling, wondering how in the world he had pulled off that magical, seemingly impossible maneuver. And the best part? The Cruyff Turn was about teaching the world a new language of movement, one where creativity was the most powerful tool.

When Cruyff executed this move, it was a statement. It said, "This is how you think your way past an opponent." It said, "This is how you outwit the opposition, not just outplay them."

It was about so much more than winning the ball—it was about creating a moment that broke the game wide open. The Cruyff Turn became more than a trick—it was a symbol of everything Johan believed in: that soccer was a game of ideas, not only actions.

Most players retire and fade away, but Johan Cruyff?

He became even MORE powerful as a coach! Cruyff wanted to change the entire philosophy of soccer, from the ground up. As a coach, he wasn't content with simply training players; he was revolutionizing how the game was understood and played. Barcelona's legendary style of play, known as tiki-taka, with its emphasis on possession and intricate passing, was pure Cruyff magic. He transformed Barcelona from a club with promise into a footballing powerhouse, blending attacking creativity with tactical mastery. And it wasn't only Barcelona that benefited from his genius—the entire world of soccer took notice of his radical approach.

Cruyff's coaching methods were not your average drills and routines. He was a philosopher, a strategist, and a visionary. Each training session was an experiment. Each tactical decision was an opportunity to push boundaries. He wanted his players to think for themselves, to become intelligent soccer players who could solve complex puzzles on the field in real-time. His coaching style was as much about mental development as it was about physical skill. His philosophy?

Players should understand the game so deeply that they can adapt to any situation.

What made Cruyff so extraordinary was his understanding of soccer's deeper layers. He knew that soccer was about more than physical prowess. It was about intelligence, creativity, and anticipation. He treated the soccer field as a complex organism, one that could be understood, manipulated, and controlled by a player with the right mindset. For Cruyff, it was never about running faster or kicking harder—it was about seeing possibilities others couldn't. It was about anticipating the next move before the ball was even passed.

He taught his teams how to play soccer and he taught them how to think. Under Cruyff, Barcelona's players weren't following instructions. They were solving problems, thinking critically, and reacting in the moment. This was the essence of Total Football—no one player was ever static, and no one position was ever fixed. It was all fluidity, adaptability, and intelligence. (His method was called Total Football because in most countries outside of America, soccer is actually called football!)

Johan was shaping his players into thinking soccer players, capable of reading the game like few others.

Cruyff's legacy was about his vision for the future of soccer. His youth academy at Barcelona became a breeding ground for world-class soccer players and world-class thinkers. He taught them how to be creative, to think critically, and to approach soccer as a life skill. Cruyff was obsessed with developing complete human beings. He wanted young soccer players to understand that the game was about growing—personally, mentally, and creatively. His youth academy was about building character, fostering imagination, and encouraging a mindset of continuous learning.

Johan Cruyff was more than a soccer icon.

He was a cultural revolution. His philosophy transcended the soccer field—it was a life approach. "Always question," he would say. "Always think differently." Cruyff believed that every person had a unique perspective, and that perspective should be nurtured and celebrated. He showed the world that soccer could be about more than winning. It could be about innovation, creativity, and pushing the limits of human potential.

His legacy was in the way he redefined what it means to be a player, a coach, and a human being. He inspired an entire generation of players and coaches to think differently, to challenge the status quo, and to believe that everything could be reinvented.

Want to unlock your inner Cruyff? Here's how champions think:

- See challenges as exciting puzzles, not obstacles.
- Never accept "that's how it's always been done."
- Trust your unique perspective and creativity.
- Practice innovation and continuous learning in everything you do.
- Believe in your ability to push beyond the limits.

Johan Cruyff proves one EPIC thing: True greatness doesn't come from following the rules—it comes from reimagining everything. Whether you dream of soccer glory or creating your own path in life, remember—greatness starts with daring to think differently, to push boundaries, and to believe in your own unique vision.

That's the Johan Cruyff story—a testament to what happens when unstoppable creativity meets revolutionary thinking!

LESSON: THE ULTIMATE SUPERPOWER THAT CHANGES EVERYTHING!

Imagine your brain as the most INCREDIBLE soccer field where ideas are players, and creativity is the ultimate championship move!

Whether you're dreaming of inventing the next big thing, solving an impossible problem, or simply finding joy in everyday moments, there's one truth you can't ignore: Creativity isn't only a skill—it's a LIFE-CHANGING SUPERPOWER!

Creativity: More Than Just a Fancy Word

Let's bust a myth right here, right now. Most people think creativity is reserved for artists or poets. WRONG! It's for anyone who dares to look at the world differently, who embraces challenges as opportunities, and who thrives on innovation!

Think about the greats: Maradona and Johan Cruyff, they rewrote the playbook for how the entire game could be understood! Creativity isn't about being flashy or perfect; it's about seeing the field, the world, or even a simple problem as something you can reimagine entirely. Picture your brain as a Swiss Army knife of innovation. Every challenge you face is another lock waiting for the perfect key—and guess what?

Creativity gives you a million keys!

When Maradona danced around defenders with his famous "Goal of the Century," he wasn't showing off. He was solving a real-time puzzle, outwitting everyone on the field with a mix of instinct, intelligence, and sheer guts. Now, imagine taking that same energy and applying it to life's challenges. Your math test? A fascinating maze to conquer. That work project? A stage to showcase your genius. Creativity lets you see beyond the obvious and craft solutions that no one else could dream of.

Johan Cruyff's Total Football: Creativity on Steroids

Here's the thing about Johan Cruyff: To him, soccer was a living, breathing system that could be bent, reshaped, and entirely reimagined! His concept of Total Football wasn't a strategy—it was a revolutionary mindset that applied creativity to teamwork, movement, and tactics in ways no one had ever considered.

He believed that players shouldn't be confined to one role, and neither should YOU. Why settle for what's expected when you can create something entirely new? Whether it's on the soccer field, in a classroom, or at work, thinking differently is your ultimate game-changer.

Unleashing Your Creative Superpowers

Want to know the not-so-secret secret of creative champions? They never accept "that's just how it's done"! Every challenge is an opportunity to break the mold and do something completely unexpected.

Strategies for Creative Thinking

Imagine your brain as a gym where creativity gets stronger with every rep. Here are your training drills:

- **Ask wild questions:** What if gravity worked sideways? What if you wrote a story from a bird's perspective?
- **Flip the script:** Take something ordinary and think of how it could be extraordinary. How would you redesign a chair to make it fun, useful, and surprising?
- **Dive into the unknown:** Don't shy away from topics or tasks that scare you. They're playgrounds for your creativity.

Academic Creativity Explosion

Think creativity is only reserved for doodling or painting? THINK AGAIN! Academic creativity is where the real magic happens.

- In science, creativity means asking questions that lead to groundbreaking discoveries. What if we could mimic photosynthesis to create sustainable energy?
- In math, it's about solving problems in ways nobody else thought of—like seeing numbers as musical notes in a symphony of equations.
- In literature, it's about writing stories so gripping they change how people see the world.

When you unleash your creative energy, every subject transforms from a task into an adventure. A physics project becomes a mission to defy the impossible. A history report evolves into a cinematic journey through time.

Everyday Innovation: The Mindset of Champions

Here's the kicker: Creativity isn't about being perfect. It's about being BRAVE. Stuck on a problem? Don't follow the rules—rewrite them! Think like Maradona dancing around defenders or Cruyff orchestrating the field like a maestro.

Your Brain: The Ultimate Innovation Machine

Every single person has creativity waiting to EXPLODE—yes, even YOU. The difference between ordinary and extraordinary isn't talent. It's belief.

Maradona didn't let his small stature stop him. Cruyff didn't accept the status quo. They turned obstacles into opportunities and used their unique perspectives to blow the world's minds.

Developing Your Creative Toolkit

Here's how to flex those creative muscles daily:

- **Ask "what if" questions:** These are the sparks that ignite innovation.
- **Challenge assumptions:** Who says socks can't have built-in heaters or notebooks can't double as puzzles?
- **Fail fearlessly:** Every mistake is a stepping stone to brilliance.
- **Celebrate your quirks:** The things that make you different are your greatest assets.
- **Stay curious:** The world is full of wonder, waiting for you to explore it.

Creativity Isn't a Gift—It's a Skill

Let's be real: Nobody is born a creative genius. Creativity is like soccer skills—you practice, refine, and repeat until you're bending reality like Beckham bends free kicks. Every day is another chance to experiment, play, and grow.

The Champions Creativity Playbook

Here's the ultimate game plan for unleashing your inner genius:

- **See challenges as adventures:** Life's curveballs are creative prompts in disguise.
- **Trust your weird ideas:** What feels "out there" today might be the next big thing tomorrow.
- **Think differently—always:** Never settle for the obvious.
- **Celebrate your perspective:** The world needs your unique way of seeing things.
- **Never stop learning:** Creativity thrives on curiosity and growth.

Creativity is the bridge between the ordinary and the extraordinary. It's about way more than being "artsy." It's about being bold enough to reimagine everything.

Whether your dream is to score the winning goal, invent a world-changing device, or simply make your day-to-day life more vibrant, the message is the same: Creativity is your superpower.

The canvas of your life is blank, and you hold the paintbrush. So go ahead: Dream big, think bold, and make some noise!

THE REAL REASON YOUR HEROES ARE HEROES

"Keep your dreams alive. Understanding to achieve anything requires faith and belief in yourself, vision, hard work, determination, and dedication. Remember all things are possible for those who believe." –Gale Devers (Olympic athlete)

There's a reason why sporting legends like the ones you're reading about here are seen as heroes—and as you might be gathering by now, it's not all to do with their performance on the court or field. Whether they're football players, basketball players, hockey players, or soccer players, they've had to overcome some serious challenges to get where they are now.

If there's one lesson to take away from all of these heroes, it's the power of perseverance in pursuing a dream. Most sporting greats have been told that they'll "never make it" at least once in their lives, and without fail, they've picked themselves up and carried on. Every time they're told they can't, they become even more determined to succeed—and that's a lesson we can all take and apply to anything we're passionate about. There's no reason you can't do anything you set your mind to. You just have to be prepared to overcome a lot of obstacles and be determined not to let any failure stop you. In fact, every failure is an opportunity to learn something and train yourself to do even better next time.

If everyone had this mindset, just think what incredible things could be achieved! You can develop that mindset, and these stories are all here to inspire you to do just that. But did you know you could make a difference to someone else's mindset too?

Simply by sharing these stories and spreading the inspiration, you could inspire other kids to chase their dreams with all the passion and dedication of the most successful athletes. One way you can do this is to tell your friends about this book, but you can take this even further by leaving a review online. If you have an Amazon account of your own, this is super easy, but if not, you can always ask your parents, your coach, or whoever bought you this book to leave one for you. Either way, the word gets out—and that can only be a good thing.

By leaving a review of this book on Amazon, you'll not only share these incredible stories that deserve to be heard, but you'll also inspire other kids to chase their dreams.

Reviews help books get into the hands of the people who are interested in them, and simply by reviewing this book and commenting on a story that particularly inspired you, you'll help other readers find out more about their favorite athletes and carry their lessons forward with them.

Thank you so much for your support. You're making more of a difference than you realize; never underestimate your power!

https://www.champlinks.com/sl/MTE4MzU=/

PELÉ AND MIA HAMM

A soccer field is a canvas where legends paint their most incredible stories! And, when some players play the game, they TRANSFORM it, turning ordinary moments into extraordinary magic that echoes through generations.

When we talk about soccer legends, we're not only discussing athletes. We're talking about world-changers who rewrote the rulebook with nothing but pure passion, incredible skill, and a spark of brilliance that makes the impossible look easy.

Take Pelé, the Brazilian wizard who grew up in a tiny town in the middle of nowhere, he turned a simple soccer ball into a ticket to global stardom. His incredible footwork was about showing kids everywhere that dreams have no boundaries. Every time Pelé touched the ball, he was proving a point: talent can emerge from anywhere, and hard work beats impossible odds. His electrifying presence on the field made soccer a universal language, bringing people together from all walks of life. He wasn't only a player; he was a symbol of hope and inspiration for millions.

Then there's Diego Maradona, the firebrand from Argentina who played with an electric energy that could light up entire stadiums. When he danced past five England defenders in his legendary "Goal of the Century," he was rewriting the art of possibility.

These pioneers set new standards by taking down existing ones! Their impact went way beyond soccer fields. They became symbols of hope, determination, and the incredible potential hiding inside every young dreamer.

When a soccer legend introduces a new playing style, they're doing something magical. Imagine a midfielder like Xavi Hernandez, who reimagined how passing could work. His style wasn't about power; it was about precision, intelligence, and creating opportunities nobody else could see.

That's a life lesson about seeing potential where others see obstacles.

The story of soccer trailblazers wouldn't be complete without celebrating the incredible women who redefined the game. Players like Marta from Brazil and Mia Hamm from the United States revolutionized it.

Marta, with her dazzling footwork and relentless determination, showed the world that women's soccer was every bit as thrilling and skillful as the men's game. Mia Hamm became an icon for her goal-scoring records and for her role in inspiring millions of girls to put on a soccer jersey and dream big.

They faced continuously challenged stereotypes, and proved that talent has no gender. Every time they stepped on the field, they were trailblazers, breaking down barriers and creating paths for the next generation. The drive to set new standards isn't confined to soccer. It's a universal superpower! Think about how a soccer player's mindset of constant improvement translates to other areas of life. Persistence, strategic thinking, and teamwork—they're life skills that can help you succeed in school, careers, and personal challenges.

When young players study these legends, they're absorbing powerful life lessons about pushing boundaries, believing in themselves, and understanding that greatness isn't about perfection—it's about passion, hard work, and the courage to be different.

These soccer heroes teach us something profound: Every dream starts with a single moment of belief.

Whether you're dribbling a ball in a dusty street or facing a challenge in your classroom, the same principles apply:

- Stay curious
- Work hard
- Never stop learning

The most incredible part?

Every single person reading this has the potential to be a trailblazer. Maybe not in soccer, but in their own unique way. The legends we celebrate didn't start as superstars. They started exactly where you are—with a dream and the desire to chase it.

Next time you see a soccer match, remember: You're witnessing a masterclass in human potential, creativity, and the incredible magic that happens when passion meets determination. Imagine this: You're the protagonist of your own soccer story. The field represents life, and the ball is your unique set of skills, challenges, and opportunities. What kind of game will you play?

The truth is, we all have a little bit of Pelé's grit, Maradona's audacity, Xavi's intelligence, and Marta's determination inside us. The trick is learning how to harness it.

Want to ignite your spark of greatness? Start with these steps:

- **Embrace challenges:** Life's curveballs are creative puzzles waiting to be solved.
- **Think differently:** The greatest breakthroughs come from breaking the mold.
- **Celebrate every win:** No matter how small, every victory fuels your momentum.

- **Stay inspired:** Surround yourself with stories of those who dared to dream big.
- **Be relentless:** Keep pushing, keep striving, and never stop believing.

This is your moment. Right now, your story is unwritten, your goals unscored, and your potential unlimited. You have the courage, creativity, and resilience to blaze your own trail.

So, whether you're kicking a soccer ball, writing a novel, building a business, or conquering a challenge, step onto that field with confidence.

PELÉ

Dreamers and doers, listen up for this story of a soccer maestro! A life journey that was a symphony of resilience, talent, and dreams that defied logic . Let's dive into the legendary life of the one, the only, Pelé: The soccer superhero who changed EVERYTHING!

Imagine a young boy in Brazil, sprinting through the sunbaked streets of Santos, his feet moving faster than his worn-out shoes could handle, a small boy not presented with many opportunities. But his dreams? Oh, those dreams were as boundless as the Brazilian sky! Pelé was a spark waiting to ignite an unstoppable wildfire.

Born Edson Arantes do Nascimento, Pelé's life began in a quiet small town setting setting. Yet, even as a child, he saw the world not as it was, but as it could be. Every street corner, every dusty alley, every makeshift soccer ball became part of his grand stage. While other kids dreamed small, Pelé dreamed big. His father, a former soccer player, inspired him with tales of the sport's beauty and potential, planting the seeds of greatness in his young mind. Pelé's early life required tenacity, determination, and imagination, as he was improvising soccer balls out of socks stuffed with newspaper. Yet, those small town beginnings became the foundation of a legacy that would transcend the sport itself.

At 15 years old, Pelé joined the Santos Football Club, and the world began to notice. Within a year, he was scoring goals like a seasoned pro. By 17, Pelé had the eyes of the world upon him as he led Brazil to a World Cup victory in 1958. Seventeen years old! Most teens are figuring out life, but Pelé was busy rewriting the rules of soccer greatness.

And what a rewrite it was. His performance in that World Cup was otherworldly. Pelé's lightning-fast footwork, unparalleled ball control, and ability to see plays unfold before they happened made him an unstoppable force. Defenders looked like extras in a one-man Broadway show.

Let's talk about his soccer skills for a moment.

Pelé was an artist, and the field was his canvas. His ability to control a ball defied physics, and his vision for the game was unmatched. Imagine defenders scrambling like chess pawns while Pelé orchestrated a symphony of soccer brilliance, every movement a perfectly executed note.

He reinvented soccer completely. Moves like the "bicycle kick" became his signature, an acrobatic masterpiece that left audiences gasping and goalkeepers hopeless. And the goals? Oh, the goals! Over 1,200 of them in official matches—a record that cements his place as a soccer deity.

But Pelé what set him apart—what truly made him a global icon—was his spirit. His glowing smile, sportsmanship, and unwavering love for the game made him a beacon of positivity. He was playing to inspire. Every time he stepped onto the field, it was as though the world paused to watch. And when Pelé played, it wasn't just Brazil cheering him on. It was kids in Africa kicking makeshift soccer balls, teenagers in Asia mimicking his moves, and families across Europe marveling at his brilliance. Pelé united the world in a way that few ever have.

Winning a World Cup is the pinnacle of any soccer player's career. Pelé didn't stop at one—he won three. His victories in 1958, 1962, and 1970 weren't only triumphs for Brazil. They were proof of the power of determination, teamwork, and pure talent.

By the time he hung up his boots, Pelé was more than a sports star. He was a national treasure. And no, that's not a metaphor. Brazil literally declared him one, ensuring he couldn't be "exported" to play for foreign clubs—a testament to his irreplaceable value to his country.

Pelé's magic didn't end when the final whistle blew. Off the field, he became a global ambassador for soccer and a symbol of hope. His story showed the world that greatness can emerge from the most unlikely places.

He worked tirelessly to promote soccer as a unifying force, traveling the globe, meeting fans, and using his platform to bridge divides.

Pelé showed us all that the game was more than a competition—it was a universal language.

Let's not sugarcoat it: Pelé's journey wasn't all smooth sailing. Growing up in a small town with less opportunities could've been a dealbreaker. Instead, it became his superpower. Each challenge was a stepping stone, each setback a lesson. He transcended his circumstances.

His story is a reminder that your background doesn't define your future. Pelé's life proves that success isn't about where you start—it's about how far you're willing to go. He showed millions of kids that with passion, hard work, and belief, anything is possible.

To this day, his story inspires generations. Kids kicking soccer balls in dusty alleys, aspiring athletes facing impossible odds, and dreamers of all kinds look to Pelé as proof that greatness knows no boundaries.

What can we learn from Pelé's incredible journey? Here's a quick playbook for life, straight from the King of Soccer:

- **Dream BIG, start small:** Pelé didn't wait for perfect conditions. He began with a ball made of socks and a dream as big as the world.
- **Resilience is key:** Life will throw challenges your way. Use them as fuel to push harder and aim higher.
- **Spread joy:** Success isn't only about personal achievements. It's about inspiring others and leaving the world better than you found it.
- **Believe in the impossible:** Pelé didn't merely aim to be good—he aimed to be the best. And he proved that with enough passion, anything is possible.

From barefoot beginnings to global fame, Pelé's story is the ultimate underdog tale. It's a story of talent, grit, and unrelenting hope. But most of all, it's a reminder that no matter where you start, you have the power to achieve greatness.

So, next time you're watching a soccer match, remember this: you're witnessing more than a game. You're seeing a celebration of human creativity, resilience, and potential—a legacy Pelé helped create.

No dream is too big, no obstacle too great, and no goal too far out of reach. So, go kick some dreams into reality.

MIA HAMM

Imagine a world where girls were told soccer wasn't their game. Then BOOM! Along came Mia Hamm, who took down those limits faster than she could score a goal!

Growing up with five brothers, Mia was proving that girls could rock the soccer field with mind-blowing skill and unstoppable determination! Her journey was about rewriting the entire playbook for women in sports!

Mia grew up in a military family, moving from base to base, but there was one constant in her life: soccer. Surrounded by brothers who challenged her at every turn, she had to keep up, but she also dominated. Picture this: a tiny Mia in a backyard, weaving past her brothers with the ball, her determination already shining brighter than a stadium floodlight. While other kids her age were playing for fun, Mia was laying the groundwork for a revolution. She was planting seeds for a future where girls could play unapologetically and dream fearlessly.

By age 15, Mia was already playing for the U.S. Women's National Team. FIFTEEN! Most of us at 15 are still figuring out how to finish our math homework. But Mia? She was making her international debut and setting the stage for a legacy that would change sports forever.

Two Olympic gold medals?

Check!

Two FIFA Women's World Cup victories?

DOUBLE CHECK!

Mia's trophy cabinet is LEGENDARY!

But here's the kicker: those trophies are shiny proof of something way bigger. Mia Hamm launched a movement that inspired millions of young girls to dream bigger!

Before Mia, women's soccer was like a tiny spark. She turned it into a blazing wildfire of excitement! Every time she stepped on the field, she was sending a message loud and clear: Girls can be absolute soccer legends!

Her stats are CRAZY impressive. Mia scored 158 international goals—a world record that stood for years! That's more goals than some entire teams manage in a lifetime. But the numbers? They don't tell the whole story. Mia was about heart, passion, and showing the world that soccer has no gender limits.

Imagine defenders scrambling, trying to keep up with her speed, her precision, and her seemingly sixth sense on the field. She was unstoppable because of her unwavering belief that she BELONGED.

Before Mia, girls in soccer often felt like an afterthought. Equipment was "one size fits all"—and by that, they meant "one size fits boys." Fields were smaller, opportunities were fewer, and visibility was practically nonexistent. When Nike created the "Mia Hamm" line of soccer gear, it was a victory for every young girl who ever dreamed of soccer stardom! She became more than an athlete—she became a global inspiration!

Mia was proof that women could be powerful, competitive, and absolutely incredible athletes. She broke down barriers, challenged stereotypes, and opened doors for an entire generation of new female soccer superstars!

Let's talk about THE moment that changed everything—the 1999 FIFA Women's World Cup. The U.S. team, with Mia at its core, played their hearts out. The final against China ended in a nail-biting penalty shootout. The world held its breath as Mia and her teammates took the stage under the pressure of millions watching.

And when Brandi Chastain's penalty shot sealed the victory?

Absolute pandemonium! But here's the thing—this wasn't about one game or one trophy. This was a watershed moment for women's sports.

The 1999 World Cup was more than a victory. It was a statement. Women's soccer was here to STAY. Stadiums filled to the brim. Television ratings soared. Little girls everywhere saw themselves as future champions. Young girls started seeing themselves differently. No longer sideline cheerleaders, they became soccer champions in their own right! Mia showed that strength, skill, and determination aren't about being a boy or a girl. They're about BELIEVING IN YOURSELF.

She embodied it. Her passion and determination became a rallying cry for girls everywhere: "If Mia can do it, so can I!"

Mia's legacy didn't end when she retired. She became a mentor, an advocate, and a symbol of empowerment. Through her involvement in charities, her work with young athletes, and her relentless push for equality, she continued to inspire.

She co-founded the Women's United Soccer Association (WUSA), the first professional women's soccer league in the U.S., giving players the opportunities Mia fought so hard for. Her autobiography, Go For the Goal, became a guidebook for aspiring athletes. And her role as a mom added a new dimension to her already extraordinary life, showing the world that women can truly have it all.

Mia Hamm's legacy is about the millions of young girls who now know they can chase ANY dream, kick down ANY barrier, and become absolute legends!

Her influence is everywhere—on every soccer field where girls play their hearts out, in every sold-out stadium cheering for women's sports, and in every young athlete who dares to dream big. Television cameras started capturing women's soccer like never before. Stadiums that were once empty became PACKED with fans. Little girls who once thought soccer was a "boy's game" now saw themselves as future world champions.

Mia's story is proof that even though change doesn't happen overnight, it does happen when someone has the courage to push forward, regardless of the odds being stacked against them.

What can we learn from Mia's incredible journey? Here's the ultimate playbook for life:

- **Dream BIG, start small:** Whether it's backyard soccer games or Olympic finals, every big achievement starts with one step.
- **Break through the limits:** Challenge the norm. Rewrite the narrative. Be the change the world needs.
- **Lift others up:** Mia didn't win for herself. She paved the way for others, proving that real success is shared.
- **Be relentless:** Mia didn't stop when she hit roadblocks. She kept going, proving that grit and determination can break through anything.

Mia Hamm TRANSFORMED it into a celebration of girl power, determination, and the incredible magic that happens when you refuse to accept limits. Her journey is proof that sports are more than games—they're platforms for change, stages for revolution, and arenas where dreams become reality.

Mia's story reminds us all that the sky's not the limit—it's just the beginning.

Who's ready to kick some DREAMS into reality?

LESSON: YOUR PERSONAL SUPERPOWER!

A legacy isn't solely about trophies or accolades. It's about the incredible impact you leave behind that keeps inspiring others long after you've left the field.

It's your unique fingerprint on the world—an eternal highlight reel that never stops playing!

Think about it: the game doesn't end when the clock runs out. Your moves, your passion, your spirit—they ripple outward, touching lives you might not even realize. Pelé, Mia Hamm, Cristiano Ronaldo, Megan Rapinoe—they're legends.

Why?

Because they TRANSFORMED the game!

When Pelé showed up from a tiny Brazilian town, he shattered the idea that your background determines your destiny. Picture this: a kid from Santos, Brazil, turning dusty streets into his personal soccer academy. Every kick of a makeshift ball—whether it was rolled-up socks or a grapefruit—was a practice shot at greatness. Pelé used soccer as a megaphone to inspire millions, showing kids worldwide that passion beats circumstances every single time. When he stepped onto the field, it was a revolution. He transformed soccer into something bigger than sport. It became a global phenomenon, a universal language, and an unshakable symbol of hope.

Every point on the scoreboard was a story. A message to every kid watching: "If I can do it, so can you!" Pelé tore up the playbook and created a masterpiece of human potential.

And then there's Mia Hamm. She bulldozed through gender barriers faster than she could score a goal! Growing up in a world where girls weren't always encouraged to play sports, Mia made sure she was UNIGNORABLE. Imagine her as a little girl, dribbling circles around her brothers, sharpening her skills with every kick. She wasn't only learning soccer. She was learning to lead. And lead she did! Two Olympic gold medals, two FIFA Women's World Cup victories, and a global fanbase that redefined the sport forever.

But here's the kicker: Mia's legacy is about the doors she kicked open for every girl who ever dreamed of lacing up her cleats. Her message was loud and clear: "Strength, determination, and skill know no gender!"

Legacy: The Power of You

So, what about YOU? You might not be Pelé or Mia (yet!), but your legacy is as important. It starts RIGHT NOW. It starts with every decision you make, every step you take, and every ounce of passion you pour into whatever you do.

Here's the BIG secret: Building a legacy doesn't mean you have to be famous. It's about making an impact—on your teammates, your friends, your community, or even that one person who needed a little spark to chase their dreams.

Dream BIG, but START SMALL!

Every incredible journey begins with a single step. Want to change the world? Start by changing your own game. Practice like crazy. Be kind. Push your limits. Show up even when it's hard. Because here's the thing: every small action is like planting a seed, and with enough care and dedication, it'll grow into something extraordinary.

Your legacy isn't about being perfect. It's about being passionate. Maybe you're the kind of player who inspires your teammates with your hustle. Maybe you're the one who cheers the loudest from the sidelines. Maybe you're the problem-solver, the motivator, the never-give-up-er. Whatever it is, those are your superpowers.

Think about it: What's your unique gift? Are you a fantastic team player? A visionary thinker? Someone who turns setbacks into comebacks? The beauty of legacy is that it's not one-size-fits-all. It's as unique as YOU.

And don't forget: Setting high standards isn't about being better than everyone else. It's about being better than you were yesterday. Every time you push yourself a little harder, every time you overcome a challenge, you're adding another awesome brick to your legacy building. You're writing a story. And stories have the power to inspire. Picture a younger kid watching you play—maybe they're on the sidelines, or maybe they're scrolling through social media. They see your grit, your heart, your never-give-up attitude, and they think, "I want to be like that."

That's legacy. It's the ripple effect of your actions. It's the chain reaction of inspiration that keeps spreading long after the final whistle.

Take it from the pros: Pelé didn't know he'd inspire millions when he kicked his first soccer ball. Mia Hamm didn't set out to create a global movement when she joined her first team. They simply followed their passion, step by step, led by their desires, and the rest unfolded naturally.

The Everyday Legacy

Here's the coolest part: You don't need to be a pro athlete to leave an AMAZING legacy. Your kindness, your hard work, your determination—those are the real game-changers. Every time you lift someone up, every time you give your best effort, every time you refuse to back down from a challenge, you're building your legacy.

Legacy isn't only about the big, shiny moments. It's in the small, everyday actions that show the world who you are and what you stand for. It's in how you treat others, how you handle setbacks, and how you celebrate successes—both yours and others.

Kicking Doubts to the Curb

Now, let's talk about doubt. Everyone has moments where they wonder, "Can I really do this?" The answer? YES, YOU CAN! Doubt is a pesky little defender trying to block your shot. Maneuver around them and take your shot anyway.

Start building your legacy today. Every pass, every practice, every moment of showing up for yourself and others is adding rocket fuel to your dreams. Remember, legacies aren't built overnight. They're the result of consistent effort, passion, and a whole lot of heart.

So, what will YOUR legacy be?

Will you be the teammate who lifts everyone up? The dreamer who proves the impossible is possible? The leader who inspires others to chase their goals?

The most INCREDIBLE part of your journey is that it's uniquely yours. Whether you're scoring game-winning goals, cheering from the sidelines, or bringing soccer's spirit into a totally different field, you have the power to make magic happen.

From the dusty streets of Brazil to the world's biggest stadiums, from backyard practices to Olympic podiums, the greatest legacies are built not by chance, but by choice.

Who's ready to change the world?

Let's GOOOOOO!

CRISTIANO RONALDO AND MARTA VIEIRA DA SILVA

Imagine soccer as the most incredible adventure where talent meets thunderous hard work! It's a TRANSFORMATION journey where ordinary players become EXTRAORDINARY legends!

Every match is like a stage, every practice a rehearsal for the grand performance that could go down in history.

Now, let's be real—natural talent is like having a slick sports car. It's flashy, it's cool, and it can get you pretty far, but dedication? That's the magic that makes that car blast past every limitation. You can have all the talent in the world, but without relentless commitment and a burning desire to keep getting better, you'll never reach your full potential. The most mind-blowing soccer stars? They aren't magically born with their skills. They're crafted through massive amounts of practice, passion, and pure unstoppable spirit!

These are the players who understand that greatness isn't handed to you—it's earned, and they're hungry for it.

Think about the greatest soccer players. Do you think Cristiano Ronaldo woke up one day and was the GOAT? Heck no. The dude practices free kicks when everyone else is chilling and when the lights are off, and the crowds are gone. It's that commitment to pushing the limits that makes him stand apart. Then there's Lionel Messi—his soccer field is his personal laboratory of magic. Messi experiments, he invents, he perfects. Every pass, every dribble, every goal is the result of endless hours on the training field. They didn't get there by accident. They put in the work.

Skill development isn't about being perfect from day one. It's about showing up, falling down, and getting back up with more fire than before! Every practice session is like adding stardust to your soccer dreams where you're sculpting yourself into the kind of player who dominates the field, who inspires teammates, who creates magic with every touch of the ball.

Now, here's the absolute real kicker: Confidence is your mental power tool! Sure, physical skills are important, but the real magic happens between your ears. Top players train more than their bodies—they train their entire universe of potential!

It's the mindset that separates the good from the great. Top-tier players visualize success before it happens, see themselves overcoming obstacles before they even face them, and most importantly, they turn every challenge into a stepping stone toward greater success. They've mastered the mental game as much as the physical one, and that's where true champions are born.

Let's talk about discipline. It's not a boring word or something to dread—it's your superhero cape! When the rest of the world is taking it easy, skill masters are making it happen. When others are taking breaks, you're the one searching for new ways to improve. That's PURE PASSION in action! And this? This is the key to unlocking your potential.

You see, your soccer journey is about becoming an incredible version of yourself. Every drill, every practice, every moment of focus is building something way bigger than soccer skills. You're building character, resilience, and unstoppable spirit! It's the mental grit you develop when you keep going even when you want to quit. It's the courage you cultivate when you step up to take that crucial penalty kick. It's the leadership you demonstrate when your team needs you most.

And here's the most mind-blowing part: These skills are LIFE SKILLS. The discipline you learn on the soccer field becomes your superpower in everything else you do—school, your future career, personal challenges, and beyond. The perseverance that pushes you to keep training through setbacks? It'll help you power through the tough times in life. The focus you develop when you're honing your technique? It'll help you excel in the classroom, at work, or in any goal you pursue. In short, the lessons you learn while chasing your soccer dreams are the same lessons that help you crush life!

Now, let's take a quick mental leap. Imagine yourself years from now. You've achieved your goals and have become someone who knows how to turn dreams into reality. Someone who understands that greatness isn't about natural talent alone. It's about commitment. It's about the daily grind, the constant quest to improve, and the unshakable belief that the only limits that exist are the ones you place on yourself. It's about waking up every day with a fire in your belly and an unrelenting desire to become the best version of YOU.

So grab those soccer boots, fire up that passion, and get ready to transform your entire universe! Your soccer journey starts NOW! The field is waiting for you to make your mark. And here's the thing—you're already a star. All you need is to put in the work, keep pushing yourself, and let your passion guide you to greatness. Because when you give everything you've got, when you push your limits and never settle for less, you'll look back one day and see that the legacy you built was about becoming the kind of person others look up to, someone who's unstoppable, no matter the odds.

Who's ready to become a skill master?!?!?!

Remember, this is the path to being the kind of person who transforms the world. It's about creating a legacy that's far bigger than any one game. This is your time to step into greatness and show the world what you're made of. When you make that commitment to be the best version of yourself, the game will follow. So get out there, hit the field, and let the world see what you're capable of!

Now, go ahead and take that first step toward your own journey of transformation. It all starts with one kick, one practice, and one day of showing up. That's how legends are born. And if you're reading this, guess what? You're already on your way to becoming one.

CRISTIANO RONALDO

Imagine a human rocket powered by pure determination! Cristiano Ronaldo is a LIVING, BREATHING INSPIRATION MACHINE that makes ordinary humans look like they're standing still!

When you look at Ronaldo, you're witnessing a person who is the embodiment of what happens when talent meets the relentless pursuit of greatness. This is a man who's set out to prove that nothing is impossible if you're willing to surpass the norm, push limits no one thought possible, and face every challenge head-on. He's a true example of what happens when you aim for the stars and refuse to settle for anything less than your absolute best.

Now, let's talk about his workout routine—because this is where the magic happens. Absolutely mind-blowing! While most people are still hitting the snooze button, Ronaldo is out there crushing fitness goals that sound like they belong in a sci-fi movie. We're talking about a guy who treats his body like a high-performance sports car—constantly upgraded and never slowing down! His commitment to physical excellence is next level. He wants to be unstoppable. And let me tell you, his body is a testament to that. Whether it's strength training, cardio, or agility drills, Ronaldo's workouts are crafted to make him a machine on the field.

There's no magic formula—only sweat, grit, and a level of discipline that few can ever replicate.

Diet? Forget pizza and burgers! Ronaldo's meals are precision-engineered nutrition bombs! Every single bite he takes is calculated to fuel him for peak performance, keeping him in top form year-round. He consumes six smaller meals a day, each packed with protein and essential nutrients, ensuring that his body is always operating at maximum capacity. He avoids sugar and alcohol like they're kryptonite! He gets help to make sure his power meals all taste amazing too! While others are indulging in comfort food, Ronaldo is fueling his body with the very best to perform at a level that's out of this world. He treats his body like a machine—and guess what?

It works.

But here's the wild part—Ronaldo is a business genius who became the first soccer player to crush the $1 BILLION mark!

Talk about a GAME CHANGER! From sponsorships to his own CR7 brand, he's winning at life. While many athletes may simply focus on their performance on the field, Ronaldo understands that success is about more than talent. It's about leveraging your platform, building a brand, and positioning yourself as a leader both in and out of the stadium. His CR7 brand has become synonymous with style, excellence, and determination. He's turned his fame into a powerhouse that extends beyond soccer, into fashion, fragrance, and lifestyle, proving that success isn't only about what you create, but also what you do with it.

And now, let's talk about his heart. In 2005, Ronaldo met a young tsunami survivor in Indonesia. He personally paid for the boy's education, showing that true champions lift others up! It's not about the spotlight or the applause; it's about the impact you make behind the scenes. Ronaldo went above and beyond to change this boy's life, setting a precedent for the type of man he is. And the story didn't stop there. Years later, that same young man signed with Sporting Lisbon—Ronaldo's former club.

Talk about a full-circle miracle!

It's moments like these that remind us that true greatness is about making a difference in the lives of others. Ronaldo proved that he's not only interested in being a legend on the field but also in the way he can uplift others, and that's a amazing kind of heroism.

When it comes to charity work, Ronaldo is absolutely incredible! He donates in a way that transforms lives. Whether it's supporting children's hospitals, funding medical treatments, or contributing to important medical research, Ronaldo's commitment to making the world a better place goes far beyond his fame. He's shown that soccer superstars can be real-world heroes. His charitable work is about giving back in a way that leaves a lasting, tangible impact. This is the heart of a true champion. The man is more than a soccer icon; he's a role model who uses his platform for something far greater than himself.

While most athletes are thinking about themselves, Ronaldo is thinking about the bigger picture. He's building schools, supporting medical research, and proving that success is about who you become along the way to the top. His journey from the dusty streets of Portugal to global superstardom is a thunderbolt of inspiration. He redefined what's possible when you combine crazy talent with an unstoppable greatness mindset.

He's shattered the idea that you're limited by where you come from, proving that if you keep the right attitude, you can achieve anything.

Every kick, every workout, every business decision he makes is a masterclass in human potential. Ronaldo is more than a soccer player—he's a living, breathing example of what happens when passion, discipline, and heart collide. Through his dedication and relentless pursuit of greatness, he's shown millions that with enough hard work, you can ABSOLUTELY crush your dreams.

It's about becoming the kind of person who inspires others to be better. It's about pushing the boundaries of what's possible and showing the world that with the right mindset, the sky's the limit.

And here's the best part—Ronaldo's story is for EVERYONE. His life is a blueprint for success in any field. Whether you're aspiring to be an athlete, an entrepreneur, or someone simply chasing a dream, Ronaldo's journey proves that nothing is impossible when you combine passion with dedication. His ability to constantly evolve, his attitude of always up-leveling, and his commitment to excellence are qualities we can all apply to our own lives.

Imagine for a second that YOU are the one chasing greatness.

You have the passion, the drive, the determination to rise above the ordinary and achieve the extraordinary. It doesn't matter if you're on a soccer field or in the boardroom—Ronaldo's story shows us that with the right mindset, the right work ethic, and the heart to make a difference, anything is possible.

It's time to take a page from the Ronaldo playbook and unleash your full potential. You have the power to crush your goals, to leave your mark on the world, and to become the superhero of your own story. It's about way more than the destination—it's about the transformation you go through along the way. So be like Ronaldo. Be relentless. Be unstoppable. And most importantly—be YOU.

MARTA VIEIRA DA SILVA

Imagine a young girl from Brazil with pure soccer magic flowing through her veins but zero female role models!

Growing up in Brazil, she didn't have the same opportunities that the boys did. What she did have, however, was an undeniable passion and a natural talent that made the world sit up and take notice. From the very beginning, Marta knew that soccer was her calling. A mission. A way to prove that the world didn't have to define her limits. She was ready to break every rule, smash every stereotype, and show the world that girls were as capable of dominating the game as boys.

Growing up in a world that told girls soccer wasn't their game, Marta said, "WATCH ME DO IT!" She played barefoot on dusty streets, turning soccer balls into her personal dream-making machines. Only a dirt patch, a ball, and a drive to change the world. In a country where soccer was—and still is—viewed as the ultimate man's sport, the thought of girls playing at the highest level was almost laughable. But her skills were so mind-blowing that people started calling her the "Pelé in Skirts"—and oh boy, did she earn that nickname!

Now, to earn a comparison to Pelé, one of the greatest soccer players of all time, you have to do more than play well. You have to redefine what greatness looks like, and that's exactly what Marta did, and continues to do, on a daily basis.

When other players zigged, Marta zagged! Her technical skills were like watching a soccer WIZARD cast spells on the field. Defenders looked like they were playing checkers while she was playing a high-level game of soccer with a chess-like strategy!! Every move she made was calculated, yet graceful; every dribble was a piece of art. She was weaving a magical tapestry of movement that left the crowd gasping. Defenders? They didn't know whether to stand in awe or scramble to catch up. Watching Marta was like watching someone defy gravity; she could move in ways that seemed impossible, making the beautiful game even more beautiful. Every kick was a statement: "Girls can rock this game!" With every pass, every goal, every perfect touch, she made sure the world understood that soccer was a game for anyone who had the skill, the heart, and the fire to play it.

Six-time FIFA Women's Player of the Year?

Yes! That's a global thunderbolt announcing that Marta was redefining what's possible! She became the first soccer player (male or female) to score in five different World Cups. MIND. BLOWN. Think about that for a second. Five World Cups. FIVE. That's legendary! Every four years, the world's best players come together, and for Marta to rise to the occasion time and time again is nothing short of miraculous. Every World Cup, she made a statement. Every match, she reminded us all why we should never count her out. And through it all, she did something even more powerful than scoring goals—she proved that women's soccer could be as thrilling, as competitive, and just as inspiring as the men's game.

Her journey wasn't about overnight success. It was about crazy determination! When doors closed, Marta kicked them down. When people said "no," she said, "WATCH ME!" She took down every single limitation!

From a young girl playing barefoot on the streets to a worldwide sensation, Marta's path was anything but easy. She had to overcome doubt, push past barriers, and ignore the doubters. And yet, every time she was knocked down, she came back stronger. Every challenge was another opportunity to show that her dream was bigger than any obstacle that could stand in her way.

Marta played for a bigger purpose. She played for every single girl who was told she couldn't do something. Her legacy is about barriers taken down and dreams unleashed! She broke records and shattered ceilings. She took the role of a soccer player and made it her own, giving countless young girls the confidence to pursue their dreams, no matter how big they seemed.

She became a beacon of hope and inspiration for a generation of athletes who saw themselves in her: determined, strong, and unafraid to step onto the world stage. Marta proved that when you follow your dreams and refuse to give up, you can change the game—for yourself and for everyone who comes after you.

She transformed women's soccer from a sideshow to a global celebration! It was no longer a sport played in the shadows. No longer was it a thing that people watched out of curiosity or novelty. Women's soccer became a worldwide phenomenon, and at the center of it all was Marta. Young girls started seeing themselves differently, they became soccer warriors. Marta showed the world that talent has no gender and no limits! It doesn't matter if you're male or female—if you have the skill, the heart, and the drive, you can succeed.

She helped erase the age-old notion that soccer was a man's game. Through her hard work, dedication, and leadership, she became the face of a new era in women's sports, an era where female athletes are no longer an afterthought but celebrated icons.

She went from a little girl with a dream to a global icon who changed the face of soccer forever. She proved that with enough passion, skill, and unstoppable spirit, you can absolutely change the world! Marta left an indelible legacy for the world to remember her by. Every time she touched the ball, she redefined the standard of excellence. She made every game a showcase of her vision, her artistry, and her unbreakable spirit.

She made history by chasing her dreams, and in doing so, gave countless young athletes the courage to chase their own.

Who's ready to Marta their life?

It's time to take a page from her playbook and start believing in your own potential. Whether it's soccer, business, or anything else you've got your eye on, this young lady's story is a blueprint for success. It's about more than hard work; it's about creating your path, refusing to let anything hold you back, and showing the world that no dream is too big to achieve.

Let's GO MARTA-STYLE!

LESSON: YOUR PERSONAL ROCKET FUEL TO GREATNESS!

Imagine practice as the secret that transforms ordinary players into soccer legends! Mastery isn't about being born perfect. It's about crushing your limits one practice at a time!

Cristiano Ronaldo and Marta didn't become superstars by accident. They obsessed over every single detail! While others slept, they practiced. While friends took breaks, they pushed harder. Their dedication was about becoming the absolute best version of themselves!

Mastery isn't limited to sports—it's the golden key to everything! Whether you're shooting for soccer stardom, acing math, or building the next life-changing app, the formula stays the same.

The Magic Formula for Mastery

Want to unlock your own superpower? Here's the game-changing playbook:

1. **Set CRAZY SPECIFIC Goals!**

   Don't say, "I want to improve." That's like saying you're going on a road trip without a map! Say, "I'm going to juggle a soccer ball 50 times by the end of the week" or "I'll study algebra for 20 minutes every evening." Specific goals are like GPS for your dreams—they tell you exactly where to go.

   People with clear, measurable goals are way more likely to succeed. So, write them down, stick them on your wall, and let them guide every single step.

2. **Embrace the STRUGGLE!**

   Here's the secret: Struggle is where the magic happens. Every mistake, every failure, every awkward first attempt is a step toward greatness.

   Cristiano Ronaldo didn't score free kicks perfectly the first time—he missed, he adjusted, and then he mastered it. Similarly, every test you fail or project you botch isn't a setback—it's data for your next epic victory! Look at every "failure" as fuel for your rocket ship.

3. **Create an UNSTOPPABLE Routine!**

   Consistency isn't boring; it's legendary. Top performers don't wait for motivation to strike—they build routines that make success automatic.

Think of your routine as your personal soccer coach. Wake up early, write down your goals, and create a schedule that keeps you focused. Track your progress, celebrate the small wins, and never, ever let excuses bench you.

When you practice every day, your dreams stop being distant fantasies and start becoming your reality.

Mental Training: Your Secret Superpower

What if I told you that you can practice without even lifting a finger? Sounds like magic, right? It's called visualization!

Close your eyes and picture this: You're lining up for a free kick. The crowd is roaring. You take a deep breath, visualize the ball curving perfectly into the top corner, and BANG—it's in.

Your brain doesn't know the difference between imagining success and actually doing it. Visualization primes your mind, builds confidence, and gives you an edge over the competition.

Pro tip: Combine visualization with real practice, and you're unstoppable!

Mastery Isn't Just for Soccer—It's a Life Skill!

Let's get real: The discipline, focus, and grit you develop while practicing soccer don't stay on the field. They follow you everywhere.

School? That math test becomes another challenge to conquer.

Work? Deadlines become a game you know you can win.

Life? Every obstacle becomes a chance to flex your mastery muscles.

When you commit to mastering one thing, you create a ripple effect that transforms everything!

The Power of Role Models

Think about your heroes—Ronaldo, Marta, Serena Williams, Simone Biles. They didn't just practice to improve their skills. They practiced to become icons.

And guess what? You can be that inspiration too. Every time you get better, you show your friends, family, and community that ordinary people can achieve extraordinary things.

You might not realize it now, but your dedication can spread to all around you. When people see you leveling up, they start believing they can achieve their dreams too.

Want to build mastery into your everyday life? Here's your game plan:

- **Schedule Your Practice Time**

  Set a specific time every day to practice your craft—whether it's soccer, math, coding, or painting. When you make practice a habit, it becomes second nature.

- **Break It Down**

  Big goals can feel overwhelming. Break them into smaller, bite-sized pieces. Want to learn five new skills? Focus on one at a time. Small wins build momentum!

- **Track Your Progress**

  Write down what you practice and the improvements you see. Seeing your growth over time is one of the BEST motivators.

- **Surround Yourself with Excellence**

  Find people who inspire you, push you, and celebrate your wins. Whether it's teammates, friends, or mentors, a strong support system can make all the difference.

- **Celebrate Every Win**

  Mastery isn't only about the finish line—it's about the journey. Celebrate every milestone, no matter how small. Scored your first goal? Nailed a tough math problem? Treat yourself!

Here's the truth about mastery: It's not about being the best in the world—it's about being the best YOU can be.

Cristiano Ronaldo didn't let people's opinions stop him. Marta didn't let her background define her limits. They chose to rise above every obstacle because they believed in their potential.

And you can too.

What separates good from great? It's not talent. It's BELIEF. Believe in your ability to grow, improve, and achieve things you never thought possible.

Your Mastery Superpowers

Mastery isn't about reaching perfection. It's about learning, growing, and becoming stronger every single day. It's about turning obstacles into opportunities and transforming challenges into victories.

Here's what mastery gives you:

- **Resilience:** You bounce back from setbacks stronger than ever.
- **Focus:** You see your goals with laser-sharp clarity.
- **Confidence:** You KNOW you've got what it takes to succeed.
- **Inspiration:** You motivate others to dream big and work hard.

The Championship Mastery Playbook

Ready to practice like a champion? Here's your playbook:

- **Set specific goals:** Clarity is your superpower.
- **Love the struggle:** It's your gateway to greatness.
- **Build routines:** Consistency is king.
- **Visualize success:** Train your brain like a pro.
- **Track progress:** Celebrate every step forward.
- **Inspire others:** Be a role model to those around you

The world is your field, and every day is a chance to play, practice, and grow.

So, grab those dreams, fire up your passion, and get ready to TRANSFORM your entire universe!

DAVID BECKHAM AND FRANZ BECKENBAUER

Leadership is about making an impact so powerful that it transforms entire teams, communities, and even dreams.

Think of the greatest leaders in soccer—icons like Sergio Ramos or Megan Rapinoe. They redefine the game. They orchestrate their teams like maestros conducting symphonies, bringing harmony, strategy, and energy to every move. But here's the thing: their leadership isn't loud or overbearing. It's inspiring. It's the kind of energy that lifts every single player to new heights, turning a group of individuals into an unstoppable force.

Leadership on the field means putting the team first, always. It's about understanding that success isn't about personal glory but about elevating everyone around you. When one player is struggling, a true leader steps in to support them. When morale is low, a leader sparks hope and determination. And when the pressure is on, a leader stays calm and focused, guiding the team through challenges like a ship's captain navigating a storm.

But here's the mind-blowing part: leadership doesn't require a special title or permission. It's not reserved for the chosen few or the naturally gifted. Leadership is a skill—a superpower—that anyone can develop. And soccer? It's the perfect place to build that skill!

Leadership on the soccer field is like a crash course in life skills that you'll carry with you forever. When you learn to lead your team, you're also learning to lead in school, at work, and in personal relationships.

Think about it. The communication skills you develop by coordinating plays and motivating teammates become invaluable when you're collaborating on a group project. The ability to stay calm under pressure—whether it's a high-stakes penalty shootout or a last-minute deadline—becomes your go-to superpower in stressful situations. And the discipline you build by showing up for your team, even when it's hard, becomes the foundation of your success in everything you do.

Soccer teaches you that leadership isn't about shouting the loudest or demanding attention. It's about actions, consistency, and heart. It's about being the person your teammates trust and look up to because they know you'll always have their back.

Great leaders aren't born; they're made. So, how do you develop the kind of leadership skills that inspire and empower?

It starts with a simple yet powerful formula:

- First, communicate like a champion. Leadership thrives on clear, honest, and supportive communication. When you listen to your teammates—truly listen—you create a bond that strengthens the entire team. Whether it's offering encouragement, giving constructive feedback, or simply being there to hear someone out, communication is the bridge that connects individual efforts to team success.

- Next, lead by example. Actions speak louder than words, and great leaders show their commitment through what they do, not just what they say. Be the first to arrive at practice and the last to leave. Give 110% effort, not because someone is watching, but because it's who you are. When your teammates see you giving it your all and showing up consistently with a positive attitude, they'll be inspired to do the same.
- Finally, embrace challenges as opportunities. Leadership is most visible when the going gets tough. Anyone can lead when things are going well, but true leaders shine when faced with obstacles. Stay calm, assess the situation, and focus on finding solutions. Every setback is a chance to learn, grow, and show your resilience.

What's incredible about leadership is how far its impact reaches. When you lead with positivity, courage, and commitment, you create a ripple effect that touches everyone around you.

Leadership isn't always flashy. In fact, the most impactful leaders often go unnoticed in the moment because they're too busy lifting others up. Maybe it's offering a kind word to a nervous teammate before a big game. Maybe it's staying late to help someone perfect their technique. Or maybe it's simply leading by example, showing up day after day with the same level of passion and dedication consistently.

But don't underestimate the power of those small actions. Over time, they add up to something extraordinary. You don't have to wait to be "officially" recognized as a leader to start leading. Every day is an opportunity to practice, to grow, and to make a difference.

Leadership isn't only a skill. It's a mindset. It's the belief that you can make a difference, no matter where you are or what you're doing. And once you've embraced that mindset, there's no limit to what you can achieve.

Now, here's the most exciting part: You don't have to wait to become a leader. You already have everything you need to start leading today!

So, are you ready to lead like a champion?

DAVID BECKHAM

There was a kid from East London with dreams bigger than the biggest stadium, who rose to soccer stardom and became a global phenomenon. David Beckham wasn't satisfied with only being good at soccer. No, he turned himself into an entire soccer universe!

Let's rewind to Manchester United, where Beckham started as a talented teenager with a laser focus and an NEXT LEVEL work ethic. While other players went home after practice, young Beckham was out there perfecting his craft, launching ball after ball into the net. Those iconic free kicks? They were art in the making!

By the time Beckham stepped onto the pitch as a professional, he was creating pure magic. Every pass, every cross, every shot seemed almost otherworldly. Fans experienced him. He became a player who could turn the tide of any match with a single moment of brilliance But being a soccer wizard wasn't enough for Beckham. Oh no, this guy had leadership written in the stars. When he became captain of the England national team, he turned the armband into a symbol of hope, resilience, and unstoppable spirit.

Every time Beckham led his team onto the field, he was carrying the dreams of an entire nation. The pressure? HA! He ate pressure for breakfast and turned it into power. Beckham wasn't the kind of leader who barked orders from the sidelines. He inspired his teammates with his passion, his work ethic, and his absolute refusal to quit.

Let me tll you about a legendary free kick against Greece in 2001. With England's World Cup qualification on the line, Beckham stepped up in the dying minutes, bent the ball into the net, and sent the whole nation into euphoria. He made the impossible look effortless.

When his playing days ended, he looked at the soccer world and thought, How can I make it even better? Enter Inter Miami CF.

Beckham decided to own a team and he set out to create a soccer revolution in the United States. His vision? To turn Miami into a soccer paradise and inspire a whole new generation of fans. From signing global superstars to building state-of-the-art facilities, Beckham poured his heart and soul into every detail.

Inter Miami CF is a movement in soccer. Beckham is proving that soccer in the U.S. can be as electrifying as anywhere else in the world. And his work is paying off—Miami is becoming a hotspot for soccer lovers, a place where the beautiful game is celebrated like never before.

Here's what makes Beckham's story so extraordinary: his leadership goes WAY beyond soccer. He's showing that true leaders use their skills to create opportunities everywhere they go.

Beckham's philanthropy is as impressive as his soccer career. From supporting children's charities to working with UNICEF as a Goodwill Ambassador, he's constantly giving back. He's proving that leadership isn't only about titles or trophies; it's about IMPACT. Whether he's in cleats or a business suit, Beckham's always asking, How can I make the world better?

What's truly mind-blowing about Beckham is how many times he's reinvented himself. Player. Captain. Global icon. Team owner. Philanthropist. Every time he takes on a new challenge, he approaches it with the same dedication and passion that made him a soccer legend.

From bending free kicks to bending the future of soccer, Beckham is proving that greatness isn't something you're born with—it's something you build through discipline, vision, and a relentless belief in yourself.

Here are a few golden nuggets of wisdom we can all learn from his journey:

1. **Turn pressure into power:** Beckham thrived under pressure. Whether it was a game-winning free kick or leading a struggling team, he used high-stakes moments as opportunities to shine.
2. **Lead by example:** Beckham was a walking embodiment of discipline. His dedication on the field inspired everyone around him to raise their game.
3. **Never stop evolving:** Leadership isn't a one-and-done deal. Beckham's ability to adapt and excel in different roles shows that true leaders are always growing.
4. **Use your platform for good:** Beckham leveraged his fame to make a difference, proving that leadership is about using your influence to create positive change.

Beckham's impact on the soccer world is undeniable, but what's even more exciting is how he's shaping its future. Every move he makes—on the field, in the boardroom, or in the community—is another chapter in a legacy that's still being written. He's proving that leadership isn't a destination; it's an ongoing journey of growth, impact, and innovation.

Ready to bend it like Beckham?

FRANZ BECKENBAUER

They called him "Der Kaiser" (The Emperor) because Franz Beckenbauer completely rewrote the rules of how the game could be played!

His brilliance wasn't all about his goals, tackles, or assists—it was also in the way he saw the game, reimagined it, and turned it into a whole new art form. Beckenbauer didn't only play soccer. He became soccer.

Beckenbauer pulled off something that sounds like a soccer fairy tale—he won the World Cup TWICE, but here's the CRAZY part: He did it once as a player in 1974, then again as a manager in 1990! That's like being the star of the show, and then coming back to direct the whole production!

Beckenbauer transformed the defender's role forever. He invented a whole new way to play defense that would forever change how the game was played—the sweeper position. Now, instead of just blocking shots and clearing the ball, he turned defense into an art form. He was; a magician who used his feet. His elegance on the ball made him look like he belonged in the midfield or up top as a forward, but no—he was back there orchestrating the play from deep.

And, while other defenders simply kicked the ball away in panic, Beckenbauer took it in stride, starting attacks from the back—he proved defenders could be playmakers too! He was so far ahead of his time that people were left scratching their heads, wondering how a defender could be so instrumental in shaping an attack. That's why they called him the Emperor: because he ruled the game.

German soccer?

He took Germany's already strong soccer foundation and added layer upon layer of brilliance. His leadership, both as a player and a manager, helped shape German soccer into a perfect blend of power and beauty. Under his watch, Germany became a force of nature, a well-oiled machine that could play with creativity and flare while still holding that trademark German discipline. Beckenbauer showed the world that greatness in soccer wasn't about one-dimensional approaches—it was about blending styles, expanding horizons, and evolving constantly.

In 2006, Beckenbauer pulled off his biggest victory yet—bringing the World Cup to Germany! This was a game-changer. The 2006 World Cup was about transforming an entire nation's image on the global stage. The whole world saw Germany as more than efficient and disciplined—it saw them as a proud, passionate soccer nation, capable of throwing one heck of a party. The 2006 World Cup turned Germany into the world's biggest soccer party! Beckenbauer brought a whole new spirit to the country. He made soccer come alive in a way that transcended the sport itself and made people feel like they were part of something bigger.

And his impact?

It goes WAY beyond winning games. Beckenbauer's leadership was about thinking bigger than the moment, about creating legacies that would last long after the final whistle blew. Beckenbauer showed us that true leaders think beyond the now and make choices that shape future generations. It was about how the game could evolve and expand to greater heights.

From the soccer field to the manager's bench to running huge tournaments, Beckenbauer proved that real leaders never stop growing!

And think about this: This guy mastered every single level of soccer! As a player, he was a legend. As a manager, he was incredible. And as an administrator, he was game-changing! Beckenbauer set a standard and he redefined what it meant to be a soccer leader. His legacy lives on in every defender who dares to play creatively, every leader who dares to dream bigger, and every person who believes that soccer can change the world.

Beckenbauer's legacy is about being an example and about what he inspired others to do. It's about changing the world, one game at a time, and proving that when you rule with vision, heart, and passion, there's no limit to what can be achieved.

That's how the Emperor of soccer changed the game—forever.

LESSON: YOUR LEADERSHIP PLAYBOOK

David Beckham and Franz Beckenbauer embodied what true leadership is all about. Let's dive into their playbooks and discover how they turned soccer into an art form, both on and off the field!

Let's kick things off with "Becks"—the man, the myth, the legend! David Beckham was famous for his jaw-dropping free kicks, for sure, but he was also a leader in every sense of the word. It wasn't just his incredible talent on the pitch that made him a global icon; it was his leadership. Beckham was the kind of guy who never let the weight of expectations drag him down—he let it fuel his fire.

When his playing days were over, he rolled up his sleeves and got to work—creating academies for young players, using his global platform for charity, and even playing a pivotal role in bringing the Olympics to London in 2012. Beckham kept leading after retirement, showing us that leadership is a lifetime commitment.

Now, let's talk about "Der Kaiser"—Franz Beckenbauer! The man won the World Cup as both a player AND a coach. Think about that for a second—no one else has ever done that. That's like winning a championship ring, retiring, and then coming back as the head coach to win it all over again. Mind-blowing, right?

But it was more than Beckenbauer's accolades that made him legendary—it was how he led his teams. His leadership was magnetic. He made tough moments seem easy, and that ability to remain unshaken? That's a skill every leader can take notes on.

He helped shape the entire culture of German soccer. His leadership was about empowering his team to reach their full potential. He led by example, and that's why his legacy continues to inspire soccer players around the world.

Lessons From Beckham & Beckenbauer: You Can Lead Too!

So, what do we take away from these two soccer legends? Well, it's simple: you don't need to be a world-class athlete to show leadership—you need the right mindset and a willingness to step up when it counts.

Beckham and Beckenbauer didn't become leaders by accident—they made decisions every day that set them apart. And guess what? You can do the same!

- **Speak Up, Stand Tall**

  Remember when Beckham lifted his teammates' spirits with a simple word or a pat on the back? That's leadership at its core—encouraging others when they need it most. Whether it's on the soccer field or in the classroom, speaking up and supporting those around you can make all the difference. So next time a teammate is feeling nervous before a big game or a friend is stressed about a test, take a page out of Beckham's book. Show them that you believe in them.

- **Be the Problem-Solver**

  Leadership is about taking action. Beckenbauer didn't wait for others to fix problems; he took matters into his own hands. If you see something that needs fixing—whether it's helping to clean up after a practice or solving a problem on the field—take charge. When you lead by example, others will follow.

- **Keep Your Cool**

  Here's a secret from both Beckham and Beckenbauer: leaders keep their cool, even when the pressure is on. It's easy to lose your temper or get frustrated, but real leaders stay calm and think through the situation. Whether you're facing a tough opponent or a difficult challenge in school, take a deep breath, stay focused, and tackle the problem head-on. Your teammates will respect you for it, and you'll be setting an example for others to follow.

Leadership Beyond Soccer: How You Can Lead In Every Part of Your Life

Now, here's the fun part: You can practice these leadership skills anywhere! Check it out:

- **In Class:**

  You don't have to be the loudest person in the room to show leadership. Help out a classmate struggling with homework, raise your hand when everyone else is too shy, or encourage others to participate in a group discussion. Every time you step up, you're practicing leadership.

- **On Your Team:**

  Show up early for practice. Help set up equipment. Thank your coach. These may seem like small actions, but they're huge when it comes to leading by example. Leaders show up, and they make the effort to make everyone else's experience better, too.

- **In Your Neighborhood:**

  Leadership is about making things happen in your community. Organize a mini-soccer tournament, start a recycling project, or help out a neighbor who might need a hand. Leadership can take place anywhere, and it starts with taking the initiative to make the world around you better.

Here's the best part of all: leadership isn't about being perfect. It's about doing your best, learning from your mistakes, and inspiring others to do the same.

You don't need a title or an armband to make an impact. You need the heart to step up, inspire others, and do what's right.

NEYMAR DA SILVA SANTOS JR. AND PAULO DYBALA

Ever noticed how a simple round ball can make kids smile in every corner of the world? From the sunny streets of Rio to the snowy fields of Norway, soccer works its magic everywhere it goes.

You see, soccer's like this amazing superpower that speaks EVERY language! Think about it—when kids kick a ball around, they don't need to speak the same words to understand each other. The game does all the talking!

Want to hear something super cool?

Right now, as you're reading this, millions of kids just like you are playing soccer. In Africa, they might be using a ball made from rolled-up socks. In South America, they could be playing barefoot on the beach. In Asia, they might be practicing in their schoolyard. But they're all playing the same beautiful game you love!

And guess what?

When these kids grow up, some of them become soccer superstars who show the whole world how special their home countries are! Take Mohamed Salah—this amazing player from Egypt doesn't only score goals for Liverpool. Every time he steps onto the field, he shows everyone the grace, skill, and determination that represents his homeland. Kids in Egypt look at him and think, "That could be me one day!"

Or look at Son Heung-min from South Korea! When he plays for Tottenham Hotspur, he's sharing a piece of Korean culture with everyone watching. His smile, his sportsmanship, and his incredible skills make people want to learn more about where he comes from.

But soccer brings entire nations together! Remember the 2010 World Cup in South Africa? It was about a whole continent coming together to celebrate! The sound of vuvuzelas became the sound of Africa sharing its joy with the world!

And speaking of the World Cup—wow! Every four years, something absolutely incredible happens. The whole planet stops to watch the same game! Billions of people—yes, BILLIONS with a B—all cheering, hoping, and dreaming together. In those moments, it doesn't matter what language you speak or what food you eat, or what clothes you wear. Everyone's a soccer fan! Soccer even helps solve big problems in our world! When teams from different countries play together, people learn about each other's cultures. They try new foods, hear new music, and make friends they never thought they'd have.

Some soccer stars use their fame to help others. Didier Drogba helped bring peace to his home country, Ivory Coast. Megan Rapinoe works to bring forth equality. These players show us that soccer can change the world!

And here's a secret—you're part of this awesome global soccer family too! Every time you kick a ball, you're connecting with millions of other kids doing the same thing. Maybe you've played soccer with someone from another country or watched a game in a different language. That's you being part of soccer's big, wonderful world!

Soccer is a game where rivalries often make us feel like we're worlds apart, but when the game is over, those same rivals become friends. Think about the massively competitive games between Argentina and Brazil—countries with a big rivalry. But when the final whistle blows, it's not about who won or lost. It's about the respect shared between the players, the fans, and the entire region. Soccer has a way of teaching us that rivalry can coexist with respect and unity.

Want to make the soccer world even more amazing? Here's how you can help:

- Learn about players from different countries - their stories will blow your mind!
- Try playing soccer games from around the world (did you know kids in some countries play with coconuts?)
- Make friends with players from other cultures - they might teach you cool new moves!
- Watch matches from different leagues around the world - each country plays with its own special style.

It's about coming together with others, regardless of where you come from, and sharing that joy. It's about meeting new people and embracing the common thread that ties us all together—the game itself!

Soccer's more than a game—it's like a giant friendship bracelet that wraps around the whole Earth! It reminds us that even though we might look different or live far apart, we're all part of the same team.

But let's talk about another way soccer brings the world together—the power of youth. In communities where opportunities are limited, soccer is often one of the few outlets where kids can express themselves, develop skills, and find their place. From remote villages in Africa to inner-city neighborhoods in Europe, soccer pitches are the great equalizers. No expensive gear required—just a ball and the determination to play.

Soccer has been used in numerous social projects around the world to help kids stay out of trouble, develop life skills, and even improve their education. Organizations like the Street Football World and Common Goal are using soccer to create positive change in communities everywhere. They're bringing hope and opportunities to kids who otherwise might never get the chance to dream big. And they're doing it all through the simple, powerful tool of soccer.

And the coolest part? There's always room for more players in this worldwide game!

So next time you're out there kicking the ball around, remember—you're part of a global family that stretches across oceans and continents.

You're sharing in the global language of soccer, and that, my friends, is a feeling like no other.

NEYMAR DA SILVA SANTOS JR.

Neymar—the boy from Brazil who dances with the ball like it's his samba partner! Whether he's weaving through defenders, flipping through the air, or making everyone in the stadium hold their breath, Neymar's got a gift that's all his own—it's the heart, the soul, and the passion he brings to the beautiful game!

Picture a tiny kid playing soccer in the streets of São Paulo, Brazil. His feet are moving so fast you can hardly follow them! That little boy? Yep, that was Neymar! Back then, he was like you—dreaming big and following passions! But this kid had something special brewing in those dancing feet of his! Something that, one day, would take him all the way to the global soccer stage.

Do you know what makes Neymar super-duper special? He's carrying on Brazil's amazing soccer story! Think of it like a beautiful book—Pelé wrote the first chapters, Ronaldinho added his own sparkly pages, and now Neymar's writing his magical tales! In Brazil, they turn soccer into art. They call it "jogo bonito"—the beautiful game.

Want to know how little Neymar became the superstar we know today?

Before he was filling up huge stadiums, he was playing futsal (that's like soccer but indoors with a smaller ball). Every flip, every twist, every rainbow kick—they all started in those futsal courts! In fact, Neymar himself says futsal helped him become the soccer player he is today. It was there he learned how to move with quick precision, master tight control of the ball, and make lightning-fast decisions that would impress on any pitch.

As Neymar grew up, people started noticing something amazing—this kid was putting on a show! When he got the ball, everyone would jump to their feet because they knew something awesome was about to happen. He'd do these moves that looked like they came straight from a video game—except this was real life! But what made him stand out was that he was expressing himself, sharing Brazil's joy and flair with the world. His style wasn't about competition—it was about bringing beauty and fun back into the game.

At Santos FC (that's the same team where Pelé played!), teenage Neymar started showing everyone what Brazilian soccer was all about. He'd do these tricks that made defenders look like they were stuck in silly putty! His signature flair with the ball became not only a symbol of his talent but also of his roots, and the culture he came from.

Then, as his talent started to shine, Neymar made the big move to Barcelona. Can you imagine? One day you're playing at Santos, and the next, you're on the same team as Messi! Wow! When Neymar made that jump, the entire soccer world held its breath. But did Neymar buckle under pressure? Nope! He brought all of Brazil's samba magic to Spain and shared it with the whole world. His famous mohawk haircut became the most-wanted style in soccer camps around the world. Talk about being a trendsetter!

But you know what's the most amazing thing about Neymar?

He never forgot where he came from! He still plays soccer with that same huge smile he had as a kid in São Paulo. When he scores a goal, he dances like he's back on those Brazilian streets, reminding us that soccer is about joy. His smile, his laughter, his playful spirit—it's all part of his magic. That's the thing about Neymar—it's never been all about him. It's been about inspiring others. He's a role model who encourages us all to have fun, be bold, and believe that anything is possible if we work hard enough.

Neymar helps lots of kids in Brazil through his special institute. He builds soccer fields in poor neighborhoods, gives out soccer equipment, and helps with education too! He remembers what it was like being a kid with big dreams, so now he helps other kids chase their dreams! Through his Neymar Jr. Institute, Neymar provides access to soccer as a tool for change and empowerment for kids who otherwise might not have the chance to pursue their dreams.

Want to play like Neymar? Here's what he'd tell you:

- Practice those fancy moves, but always keep smiling!
- Work hard, but make sure you're having fun too!
- Be creative—try new tricks and don't be afraid to mess up!
- Share your love of the game with everyone around you!

Neymar proves that soccer is about more than playing well. It's about spreading joy, sharing cultures, and embracing the beauty of the game. Every time Neymar steps onto the field wearing Brazil's famous yellow jersey, he's playing for every kid who's ever kicked a ball in the streets of Brazil. He's playing for everyone who believes soccer should be beautiful and fun!

Keep practicing those moves, and always remember—like Neymar shows us, the best soccer comes from a happy heart!

PAULO DYBALA

You're about to hear the amazing story of Paulo Dybala—the boy from tiny Laguna Larga, Argentina, who became one of soccer's brightest stars!

Little Paulo wasn't born into a fancy soccer academy—nope! He was a kid with a ball, a big dream, and a family who believed in him. His dad would watch him practice for hours in their yard, probably thinking, "This kid's got something special!"

But here's where it gets SUPER interesting! In Argentina, soccer is like breathing! Kids play it everywhere, all the time. And Paulo? He soaked up every minute of it! He'd practice these amazing moves that would make grown-ups stop and stare. When he scored goals, he'd celebrate by putting on an imaginary mask—yes, that's where his famous "Dybala mask" celebration came from! But life wasn't always easy for young Paulo. When he was 15, something really tough happened. His dad, who was his biggest fan, passed away. But instead of giving up, Paulo played even harder! He knew his dad would want him to keep chasing his soccer dreams. How brave is that?

Soon, Paulo was playing for Instituto in Córdoba—his first real team! At Instituto, Paulo's passion for the game was clear. He was putting on a show! The way he dribbled, the way he weaved through defenders, it was like watching an artist at work. Even though the ride to training was long, Paulo's heart was always full of energy, and that love for the game shone through in every move.

Then came the BIG jump—all the way across the ocean to Italy! Imagine leaving everything you know—your family, friends, favorite foods—to play soccer in a country where you don't even speak the language! That's what Paulo did when he joined Palermo.

In Italy, Paulo became known as "La Joya"—The Jewel! And boy, did he shine! When he moved to Juventus, he got to play with his hero, Cristiano Ronaldo! Think about that—from watching soccer stars on TV in his small town to playing right next to them! Dreams were truly coming true.

But Paulo never forgot where he came from. Every time he scores and puts on that mask celebration, he's showing kids back in Argentina that their dreams can come true too! When he puts on the blue and white striped jersey of Argentina's national team, he's playing for every kid kicking a ball in the streets of South America!

Now at Roma, Paulo's still making magic happen. He's learned to mix his Argentine soccer style with Italian soccer smarts. It's like he's created his own special soccer recipe—blending the best of both worlds and showing the world that there's no one quite like him!

He shows us that you don't need to start in a fancy soccer academy to become great. You need:

- A big dream in your heart
- The courage to work super hard
- People who believe in you
- And most importantly, the joy of playing the game!

Every time Paulo steps onto the field, he carries a piece of Laguna Larga with him. When kids in his hometown watch him play on TV, they see themselves in him.

Want to be like Paulo? Here's what his story teaches us:

- Practice your moves whenever you can (even in your backyard!)
- Don't be scared to try new things (like moving to a new team or learning
- Keep your family and hometown in your heart
- Create your special way of playing!

Paulo's also super kind off the field—he helps kids in Argentina get soccer equipment and supports his old neighborhood. Because being a great soccer player is about making other people's dreams possible too!

Every time you see Paulo do his mask celebration, remember—that's not just a soccer player scoring a goal. That's a little boy from Laguna Larga showing the world that soccer dreams really do come true!

LESSON: MAKING FRIENDS AROUND THE WORLD!

Remember how Neymar brought his Brazilian samba style to Spain and France? And how Dybala packed his Argentine magic and took it all the way to Italy? That's what we call cultural exchange—it's like a giant show-and-tell where everyone shares the most awesome parts of their home with new friends!

But here's the super exciting part—you don't need to be a famous soccer player to share your culture with others! You've got your own special way of making the world more colorful and fun. Want to know how? Check this out:

- Love playing sports? Try learning games from different countries! Did you know kids in Thailand play takraw? Like volleyball, but you can only use your feet. Or that in Afghanistan, they play buzkashi on horseback? Each game tells us something amazing about that country's history and people! And guess what? By learning these games, you're already becoming a cultural ambassador, like Neymar and Dybala! You're sharing a story.
- Maybe music's your thing? Awesome! Learn songs from around the world. When Neymar hums Brazilian samba tunes during warm-ups, he's sharing a piece of his homeland. You could start a world music club at school—imagine having a playlist that travels around the globe! You might end up humming a French chanson one minute, and a Nigerian Afrobeats hit the next!
- Food fan? Even better! Every dish has a story to tell. When Dybala learned to love Italian pasta, he was learning about Italian family traditions. Maybe you could organize an international food day in your class. Imagine the fun you'd have trying dishes from India, Japan, Italy, and beyond. Each bite would bring you closer to understanding another culture.

Here's something that'll blow your mind: every time you share something from your culture, you're being like Neymar and Dybala! When you teach a friend your favorite game or show them how your family celebrates special days, you're spreading your culture. And guess what happens when we share our cultures? We discover that we're all way more alike than different!

Want to be a world-connecting superstar? Here are some moves you can try:

- Start a collection of games from different countries and teach your friends how to play!
- Learn to say "hello" in as many languages as you can – it's like having a secret code to unlock new friendships!
- Try cooking dishes from around the world with your family – who knows, you might discover your new favorite food!
- Make friends with kids who come from different places and ask them to share their favorite traditions.

- Share your favorite traditions and ask others about theirs – it's a recipe for connection!

The cool thing is, when you open your heart to other cultures, amazing things happen! Ask Neymar—he probably never thought Brazilian soccer moves would make French kids dance with joy. Or ask Dybala—bet he didn't expect Italian grandmas to be making him home-cooked meals! These players may have brought their games to new lands, but they also brought new friends and memories with them. And that's what sharing culture does—it builds bonds, breaks down barriers, and makes the world feel a little smaller and a lot more friendly.

Every time you learn something new about another culture, it's like adding a new color to your crayon box—suddenly, you can draw even more beautiful pictures! Maybe you'll discover a new hobby, like learning the flamenco dance from Spain, or find a new sport you want to try. Maybe you'll even make a new friend from the other side of the world, who will show you a whole new way of looking at things. Who knows?

And here's the most wonderful part—when you share what makes you special, and others share what makes them special, we create this beautiful mix of awesome things! It's like making the world's biggest, most colorful friendship bracelet! Think about it: Neymar brought Brazilian joy to Europe, Dybala brought Argentine passion to Italy, and YOU can bring your own special something to the world too! Maybe you'll teach your friends your grandmother's special dances, share your favorite celebration songs, or show them how your family plays games!

The world's waiting for your flavor!

THE FINAL WHISTLE: YOUR SOCCER JOURNEY BEGINS

You know those amazing soccer stories we've been talking about? They're not just about fancy footwork and winning trophies—they're secret playbooks for YOUR life!

Think about Neymar. Before he was dazzling the world with jaw-dropping moves, he was just a kid with a dream and a soccer ball. Sound familiar?

Maybe you're dreaming of becoming a doctor, an artist, or a soccer star! The cool thing is, you can use the same superpowers these heroes used to chase YOUR dreams!

Let's peek into the playbooks of our heroes:

- **Be Brave Like Beckham**

  Remember how David Beckham kept taking free kicks even after missing some big ones? That's bounce-back power! Whether you're tackling a tough math problem or learning a new sport, sometimes you'll miss. But here's the secret: every time you try again, you're getting stronger!

- **Practice Like Pelé**

  Did you know Pelé used to practice with oranges and rolled-up socks when he didn't have access to a real ball? Maybe you don't have the fanciest supplies, but you have something better—your imagination! Use what you have, and make it magical!

- **Team Up Like Messi**

  Even Messi needs his teammates! When you're working on a project or learning something new, don't be afraid to pass the ball to your friends, teachers, or family. Sometimes the best goals come from awesome teamwork!

Now, let's start writing your success story:

- **Make Your Game Plan**

  Like soccer players plan their moves, write down your big dreams! Want to get better grades? Learn to play guitar? Make the school team? Writing it down makes it real!

- **Practice Your Moves**

  Set aside "training time" each day. Whether it's 30 minutes of reading or an hour of practice, even small sessions add up to BIG improvements!

- **Create Your Highlight Reel**

  Keep track of your wins big and small! Did you finish your homework early? Victory dance! Every success is like scoring a goal in your personal championship!

Your path doesn't have to look like anyone else's. Some players are fast like Mbappé, others are clever passers like De Bruyne. YOUR story will have its flavor—and that's what makes it awesome!

When things get tough (and they will), remember this: every soccer superstar had moments when they wanted to quit. But they didn't. They kept going, and so can you! Every challenge is a chance to show your strength and perseverance.

Help Others Along the Way

While you're working on your dreams, help others with theirs! Maybe you could:

- Help a classmate
- Cheer on a friend
- Share your skills
- Encourage someone who needs it

Like in soccer, life's biggest victories are even better when we help others succeed!

Every day is a chance to add another awesome chapter to your story. Maybe today you'll:

- Try something that scares you a little
- Help someone who needs a boost
- Learn from a mistake and come back stronger
- Take one step toward your dream

The best part? Every day brings new chances to shine! Your story isn't only about reaching one big goal—it's about all the amazing things you do along the way!

So tie those shoes tight, hold your head high, and get ready to make magic happen! Your story is beginning, and it's going to be AMAZING! Keep pushing, keep dreaming, and most importantly—keep believing in yourself!

Your game, your rules, your amazing story—it's all waiting for you to make it happen!

SHARE THESE STORIES!

Every time you start to doubt yourself or your confidence takes a knock, remind yourself of these inspirational tales. Self-belief is a powerful thing, and every one of these athletes has it. Share their stories now to inspire even more people like you!

Simply by sharing your honest opinion of this book and a little about your favorite story, you'll keep these incredible tales alive, and you'll help other kids find them and feel as inspired as you do right now.

Thank you so much for sharing these stories and leaving a review. They deserve to be heard!

https://www.champlinks.com/sl/MTE4MzU=/

REFERENCES

Andriote, J.-M. (2022). *What does it mean to leave a legacy?* Psychology Today. https://www.psychologytoday.com/intl/blog/stonewall-strong/202209/what-does-it-mean-leave-legacy

Armstrong, K. (2019). Carol Dweck on how growth mindsets can bear fruit in the classroom. *APS Observer, 32*(9). https://www.psychologicalscience.org/observer/dweck-growth-mindsets

Augustyn, A. (2019). Marta | Biography & facts. In *Encyclopædia Britannica*. https://www.britannica.com/biography/Marta

Boyles, M. (2022, February 1). *What is creative problem-solving & why is it important?* Business Insights Blog. https://online.hbs.edu/blog/post/what-is-creative-problem-solving

Britannica. (2018). Pele | Biography, world cups, & facts. In *Encyclopædia Britannica*. https://www.britannica.com/biography/Pele-Brazilian-athlete

Carol Dweck: A summary of the two mindsets. (2015, March 2). Farnam Street. https://fs.blog/carol-dweck-mindset/

Cassingham, S. (2024, March 4). *What does it mean to leave a legacy?* Medium. https://medium.com/@stevecassingham/what-does-it-mean-to-leave-a-legacy-de3cad597b05

Christian Pulisic. (2021, October 4). Wikipedia. https://en.wikipedia.org/wiki/Christian_Pulisic

Christian Pulisic - Player profile 24/25. (2023). Transfermarkt.com. https://www.transfermarkt.com/christian-pulisic/profil/spieler/315779

Cohn, P. (2014). *Sports visualization for athletes.* Peaksports.com. https://www.peaksports.com/sports-psychology-blog/sports-visualization-athletes/

Dealing with responsibility. (2021). M&G Skills for Life. https://www.mandg-skillsforlife.com/working-others/dealing-responsibility

Dennison, K. (2023, April 13). The importance of upskilling and continuous learning In 2023. *Forbes.* https://www.forbes.com/sites/karadennison/2023/04/13/the-importance-of-upskilling-and-continuous-learning-in-2023/

El3v4tion. (2024, March 8). *Uniting the world one goal at a time: The universal language of football.* Medium. https://medium.com/@el3v4tion/uniting-the-world-one-goal-at-a-time-the-universal-language-of-football-44197d794fdc

http ://ksiefken.word…, ksiefken W. (2013, September 1). *Plus-sport: The impact of a cross-cultural soccer coaching exchange.* Journal of Sport for Development. https://jsfd.org/2013/09/01/plus-sport-the-impact-of-a-cross-cultural-soccer-coaching-exchange/

IMD. (2022, August 16). *The 8 key leadership skills you need to know in 2024.* Www.imd.org. https://www.imd.org/blog/leadership/leadership-skills/

Jamal Musiala. (2024, April 20). Wikipedia. https://en.wikipedia.org/wiki/Jamal_Musiala

Jamal Musiala | FC Bayern München | Player profile | . (n.d.). The Official Bundesliga Website. https://www.bundesliga.com/en/bundesliga/player/jamal-musiala

Joffe, P. (n.d.). *Creativity and decision making in sport: A house that can withstand a storm.* Sport Science Support. https://www.sportsciencesupport.com/creativity-decision-making-sport-build-house-can-withstand-storm/

Knight, R. (2024, October 18). *6 Essential Leadership Skills — and how to develop them.* Harvard Business Review. https://hbr.org/2024/10/6-essential-leadership-skills-and-how-to-develop-them

Maderer, D., Holtbrügge, D., & Schuster, T. (2014). Professional football squads as multicultural teams. *International Journal of Cross-Cultural Management, 14*(2), 215–238. https://doi.org/10.1177/1470595813510710

Manage expectations so they don't manage you. (2015, April 4). Alli Worthington. https://alliworthington.com/manage-expectations-so-they-dont-manage-you/

Markovic, I. (n.d.). *What is continuous learning?: Importance & benefits.* EduMe. https://www.edume.com/blog/continuous-learning

Marr, B. (2022, July 26). 10 Most important leadership skills for the 21st-century workplace (and how to develop them). *Forbes.* https://www.forbes.com/sites/

bernardmarr/2022/07/26/10-most-important-leadership-skills-for-the-21st-century-workplace-and-how-to-develop-them/

Marta (footballer). (2022, March 25). Wikipedia. https://en.wikipedia.org/wiki/Marta_(footballer)

Mind Tools Content Team. (2023). *Creative problem solving*. MindTools. https://www.mindtools.com/a2j08rt/creative-problem-solving

Paulo Dybala. (2022, January 29). Wikipedia. https://en.wikipedia.org/wiki/Paulo_Dybala

Paulo Dybala - Player profile 24/25. (2022). Transfermarkt.com. https://www.transfermarkt.com/paulo-dybala/profil/spieler/206050

Pumerantz, Z. (2024). The 100 best sports quotes of all time. Bleacher Report. https://bleacherreport.com/articles/910238-the-100-best-sports-quotes-of-all-time.

Quinn, E. (2021, July 4). *Visualization and mental rehearsal can improve athletic performance*. Verywell Fit. https://www.verywellfit.com/visualization-techniques-for-athletes-3119438

Raghad Almuntashiri. (2024, March 2). *The power of inspiration*. Medium. https://medium.com/@raghad.almnt/the-power-of-inspiration-c5d5a895d791

Rollin, J. (2018). Lionel Messi | Biography & facts. In *Encyclopædia Britannica*. https://www.britannica.com/biography/Lionel-Messi

Rollin, J. (2019a). Cristiano Ronaldo | Biography & facts. In *Encyclopædia Britannica*. Encyclopædia Britannica. https://www.britannica.com/biography/Cristiano-Ronaldo

Rollin, J. (2019b). Neymar | Biography & facts. In *Encyclopædia Britannica*. https://www.britannica.com/biography/Neymar

Schaffner, A. K. (2020, September 16). *Perseverance in psychology: 4 activities to improve perseverance*. Positive Psychology. https://positivepsychology.com/perseverance/

Soccer's global impact: How the sport influences economies and cultures. (n.d.). Maygrove College Athletics. https://www.marygrovemustangs.com/soccers-global-impact-how-the-sport-influences-economies-and-cultures.html

The Editors of Encyclopedia Britannica. (n.d.-a). *David Beckham | Biography, teams, & facts*. Encyclopedia Britannica. https://www.britannica.com/biography/David-Beckham

The Editors of Encyclopedia Britannica. (n.d.-b). *Franz Beckenbauer | German soccer player*. Encyclopedia Britannica. https://www.britannica.com/biography/Franz-Beckenbauer

The Editors of Encyclopedia Britannica. (2018). Diego Maradona | Argentine soccer player. In *Encyclopædia Britannica*. https://www.britannica.com/biography/Diego-Maradona

The Editors of Encyclopedia Britannica. (2019). Johan Cruyff | Biography & facts. In *Encyclopædia Britannica*. https://www.britannica.com/biography/Johan-Cruyff

The power of perseverance: Insights from neuroscience and psychology research. (2023, November 14). Brainfirst Institute. https://www.brainfirstinstitute.com/blog/the-power-of-perseverance-insights-from-neuroscience-and-psychology-research

Tikkanen, A. (2019). Mia Hamm | Biography & facts. In *Encyclopædia Britannica*. https://www.britannica.com/biography/Mia-Hamm

Tim Howard. (n.d.). U.S. Soccer Official Site. https://www.ussoccer.com/players/h/tim-howard

Tim Howard. (2022, September 25). Wikipedia. https://en.wikipedia.org/wiki/Tim_Howard

Wikipedia Contributors. (2019a, January 26). *Pelé*. Wikipedia; Wikimedia Foundation. https://en.wikipedia.org/wiki/Pel%C3%A9

Wikipedia Contributors. (2019b, February 6). *Lionel Messi*. Wikipedia; Wikimedia Foundation. https://en.wikipedia.org/wiki/Lionel_Messi

Wikipedia Contributors. (2019c, February 20). *Neymar*. Wikipedia; Wikimedia Foundation. https://en.wikipedia.org/wiki/Neymar

Wikipedia Contributors. (2019d, February 24). *Cristiano Ronaldo*. Wikipedia; Wikimedia Foundation. https://en.wikipedia.org/wiki/Cristiano_Ronaldo

Wikipedia Contributors. (2019e, May 27). *Franz Beckenbauer*. Wikipedia; Wikimedia Foundation. https://en.wikipedia.org/wiki/Franz_Beckenbauer

Wikipedia Contributors. (2019f, May 31). *David Beckham*. Wikipedia; Wikimedia Foundation. https://en.wikipedia.org/wiki/David_Beckham

Wikipedia Contributors. (2019g, September 21). *Mia Hamm*. Wikipedia; Wikimedia Foundation. https://en.wikipedia.org/wiki/Mia_Hamm

Wikipedia Contributors. (2019h, October 20). *Diego Maradona*. Wikipedia; Wikimedia Foundation. https://en.wikipedia.org/wiki/Diego_Maradona

Wikipedia Contributors. (2019i, December 19). *Johan Cruyff*. Wikipedia; Wikimedia Foundation. https://en.wikipedia.org/wiki/Johan_Cruyff

IMAGE REFERENCES

Freepik. (2024). All images supplied by Freepik - Free Graphic resources for everyone. Freepik. https://www.freepik.com/

Printed in Dunstable, United Kingdom

70607157R00068